HOW TO
MAKE
MONEY
ON
FORECLOSURES

By Denise L. Evans
Attorney at Law

SPHINX® PUBLISHING
AN IMPRINT OF SOURCEBOOKS, INC.®
NAPERVILLE, ILLINOIS
www.SphinxLegal.com

First Edition: 2005

Published by: **Sphinx® Publishing, An Imprint of Sourcebooks, Inc.®**

<u>Naperville Office</u>
P.O. Box 4410
Naperville, Illinois 60567-4410
630-961-3900
Fax: 630-961-2168
www.sourcebooks.com
www.SphinxLegal.com

This publication is designed to provide accurate and authoritative information in regard to the subject matter covered. It is sold with the understanding that the publisher is not engaged in rendering legal, accounting, or other professional service. If legal advice or other expert assistance is required, the services of a competent professional person should be sought.

From a Declaration of Principles Jointly Adopted by a Committee of the
American Bar Association and a Committee of Publishers and Associations
This product is not a substitute for legal advice.

Disclaimer required by Texas statutes.

Library of Congress Cataloging-in-Publication Data
Evans, Denise L.
  How to make money on foreclosures / by Denise L. Evans.-- 1st ed.
    p. cm.
  Includes index.
  ISBN 1-57248-520-5 (pbk. : alk. paper)
  1. Real estate investment. 2. Foreclosure. I. Title.

HD1382.5.E97 2005
332.63'244--dc22
                                       2005019418

Printed and bound in the United State of America.
BG — 10 9 8 7 6 5 4 3 2 1

Dedication

This book is dedicated to my husband, Bill, who taught me everything I know about real estate, but as he's fond of telling me, didn't teach me everything he knows. Thank you, Bill, for opening an exciting new world for me.

Thank you to my teachers, beginning with Miss Morgan in the 1st grade all the way through Professor Harry Cohen and the last final in the last year of law school. You taught me to look for exciting new worlds.

Contents

Introduction

I don't know about you, but I usually hate reading book introductions. Most times, it's the part where the author tries to establish a relationship with you before they lapse into dry, formal writing about their subject. I'm different—I want my book to feel like we sat down, drank some coffee together, and chatted about what I've learned over the years.

That's my goal. I love investing in real estate, talking about real estate, and sharing war stories about real estate. My hope is you'll feel the same after you've done a few deals using the ideas in my book.

With that said, here's the purpose of my introduction—housekeeping. I do things in a certain way throughout the book. It's easier if I can explain them here so we don't have to keep getting sidetracked as these issues come up later.

First, there is not one hour in the day that goes by without me checking my computer for some piece of information I need *immediately*. My primary source of information is the Internet. I'm assuming most people operate the same way, or would if they knew what words to use in a *search string*. Sometimes I'll refer you to websites if I'm reasonably confident they'll be around for a while. If I'm not sure, I'll tell you the words to search in order to come up with websites. If you need something specific to *your* state, I'll use the word "state" in the string, but I mean for you to substitute your state's name.

For those of you without convenient Internet access, or who like to do things the traditional way, I've given you a lot of resources to help you get information. Many of them involve asking the right people the right questions. Don't be bashful. Also remember that a dozen still-warm Krispy Kremes or Dunkin' Donuts go a long way towards loosening tongues and mellowing out attitudes. If anybody brings me a hot, glazed doughnut in the morning, I'll happily spill my guts on any subject.

My second housekeeping item is vocabulary. It gets incredibly boring writing about mortgages and having to use the word "lender" in every third sentence. Sometimes I'll say "banker," even though it's not just banks that loan money on real estate. In addition, I might use "owner," "borrower," or "seller." They're all the same people.

Mortgages are the same thing as *deeds of trust*, except for technical legal details that usually aren't relevant to this book. I just call them "mortgages" throughout. I know, if I were consistent and wanted to mix things up to keep them interesting, I'd sprinkle a few "deeds of trust" around to keep from using the same word all the time. On the other hand, I grew up in a state with "mortgages,"—"deed of trust" sounds weird to me.

Next is systems and procedures. I'm a big believer in doing things in a certain way, every time. Please follow the advice in this book about setting up your systems and procedures. It'll save you a lot of grief, make everything easier, and allow you to look at more deals. I have provided several forms, worksheets, and checklists to help you get started with your own systems and procedures.

The fourth big introductory point is—nothing is "Always." I've done my best to edit my book and stick in all the required words like "usually," "generally," "most times," and the rest. I probably didn't do it enough. Please take it as an article of faith that whatever I say about anything in this book, there will be exceptions.

Finally, the laws in every state are different. Not only that, but they change pretty quickly. Check the law in your state on the different issues mentioned in this book. Better yet, partner with a lawyer—they usually have money to invest and the ability to borrow lots more, but no time to find good deals.

One resource you can use to check for this information is my website, **www.moneyinforeclosures.com**. I have way too much to share to fit into one book and so I have added everything I can think of to help you on my site.

I guess that about wraps up what you need to know before you start reading. I hope you have fun, learn a lot, and go out into the world well-prepared to invest in foreclosure properties or to find and buy your dream home.

Thank you for reading my book.

Denise

Choose to Be a Hero

For ordinary Americans, the road to personal wealth and security has always been through real estate. Because of this love affair with real estate, some people rush into ownership unwisely, taking on more debt than they can afford. Sometimes when this happens, they struggle for several years, always robbing Peter to pay Paul, but still managing, in the end, to pay the bills. Other times, they simply cannot juggle the bills and foreclosure looms.

No matter how their circumstances came about, they are going to lose a valuable piece of real estate. Someone else is going to buy it at a bargain price. It might as well be you. If handled properly—with compassion and honesty—then all parties can emerge with dignity, some economic gain, and a better future.

This is where you come in. I want you to truly understand your role in the foreclosure process and to see that you have the ability to be a hero, a champion, a doer of good deeds, *and make money* or *find a personal home of your own.*

In order to feel good about the things I am going to show you and about embarking on your journey to personal security through real estate acquisitions, you have to see life through the eyes of someone facing the loss of their own dreams. If your life has been relatively stress-free, then take my word for it—people threatened with the loss of their property, their dreams, their safety, are usually paralyzed with self-recrimination, fear, anger, and isolation. Your job is to cut through all of that, and give them knowledge, courage, hope, and dignity.

- ◆ *Knowledge* regarding what to expect, so that fear of the unknown isn't added to their other burdens.
- ◆ *Courage* to face the problem and make responsible decisions regarding the best path.
- ◆ *Hope* that, although something bad is happening, it isn't the end of the world.
- ◆ *Dignity* in the understanding this could happen to anyone, and the measure of a person's worth does not come from their disasters, but in how they're confronted.

Of course, in doing this, you still can make money in the process.

If this sounds hokey to you, then you have the wrong attitude. Handled properly, you will be a hero, just like the other professionals who rise to the challenge of helping others manage and control crises.

You are going to be a trained professional when you finish this book, follow the advice in it, and put into practice the tools and habits that will lead you down the road to personal wealth and security. Even if your goal is only for one property (a personal residence) you'll still be a trained professional.

Become a Professional

As a professional, you need a name for yourself—something similar to doctor, lawyer, network engineer, or electrician. I would suggest that your name for yourself is *workout specialist*. Workout specialists all have in common the Four R's:

- ◆ Reduce debt or debt service (by sharing knowledge)
- ◆ Remove anxiety (by giving courage to act)
- ◆ Restore respect (and with it, hope and dignity)
- ◆ Receive a fair compensation in return

As a workout specialist, you will help liquidate real estate assets in order to reduce debt, remove anxiety, restore hope and dignity, and receive a fair compensation in return. There's nothing strained about that.

> **Insight:**
> I'll let you in on a secret—most people fail at buying and selling fore-closures because they feel guilty about it. Done properly, you should be proud—not ashamed.

Even if your only goal is to find a home that you can buy at a discount for yourself, you will be *no less of a workout specialist* by the time you read this book and put it into practice. You'll be able to find and purchase that dream home using the concepts and techniques in this book. Then, even if you never buy or sell another piece of property, you'll still be able to give advice to friends and relatives, or provide encouragement to someone who wants to enter this field as a moneymaking venture. I'm willing to bet that once you see how easy this is, you will use the same principles to buy newer or larger homes over the years, and perhaps even to accumulate a few rental properties to provide for your children's college education and for your retirement years.

Help Others

An important key to your success is recognizing when people can be helped by your specialty and when they might need to see some other specialist like a bankruptcy lawyer.

Good professionals with good reputations aren't greedy. They don't try to grab every single passerby and turn them into a customer or client. Successful professionals aren't stupid either. They don't waste a lot of time trying to solve problems with their particular specialty when it is never going to work. By learning to recognize the *symptoms* that might require another type of special-ist, you can make a meaningful recommendation for someone else.

Why make recommendations? Besides being helpful and costing you nothing, it gives you legitimacy. Face it, everybody knows that the doctors, lawyers, accountants, plumbers, electricians, and auto mechanics all know their colleagues in town, and what's good and bad about each one. Being willing to make a referral to another workout specialist helps establish you as a member of that community. An added benefit is that these other people will refer business to you if they're not able to help someone by their particular specialty.

Your First Steps

Right now, the only thing you have to do is practice thinking about yourself as a trained professional—a workout specialist. As a professional, you need business cards. People just don't think you are legitimate without them. Decide the information you want to appear on your business card. I would suggest your name, the title "Workout Specialist—Real Estate," a cell phone number, and an email address.

Get Focused

Whether you are looking for a personal residence or an investment, you need to set up some parameters. If you don't know how much something will cost, you don't know if you can afford it or not. You have to prepare a budget.

Your budget will help you in many ways. It will focus your thoughts on the steps involved in meeting your goals. It will help you remember what types of things you need to document, so you can write them off your taxes as business expenses. It will also help you determine what can be performed by other people and whether it makes sense to pay someone to perform particular chores, such as gathering names and addresses of potential referrers.

Some of the things you should budget for include the following.

♦ It will cost money to set up a *data management system*—either software or some sort of paper filing system. Be sure to include the *time* necessary to set everything up and to learn how to use software.

- You will have to spend time identifying possible referrers.
- You will have to spend money on paper and postage sending letters to referrers.
- There is a cost for the mileage and time you spend visiting with referrers.
- You will want to invest in thank-you cards and postage.
- Seminars will have expenses as well—preparation time, seminar time, and the cost of a meeting room. (Many times you can get meeting rooms free at your Chamber of Commerce, community college, or church.)
- Snail-mail newsletters will cost you preparation time, plus the cost of paper, printing, and postage.
- There is no monetary expense for email newsletters, but you MUST keep some indication in your files that the person has given you permission to send email. Otherwise, you're a *penny-ante spammer*.
- It will cost money to place ads in a community newspaper or thrift paper.
- You will have to spend time scoping out foreclosures and other legal notices or filings.

You might want to periodically compare your actual expenses—time and money—against what you *thought* they would be when you made your budget. That way, you can make changes if necessary.

Keep Track of Information

Even if you're doing this just to buy a personal residence and nothing more, you still need to be as efficient as possible. Doing so will enable you to look at a lot more properties and find the one that is best for you, instead of settling for what you're able to track on top of your head. Plus, things start to get confusing when you're looking at several properties. I don't want you to get confused and discouraged—you really can do this, but you need to be organized.

Systems and Procedures

I'm a big believer in systems and procedures. A *system* is a way of doing things so you don't waste time. A *procedure* is a task that gets done every time, without fail, and fits into your system in a certain way. Three-ring binders with tabbed dividers, file folders in a plastic tub, and computer programs set up in a certain way—are all systems. For example, my systems usually involve putting a person's name in Microsoft Outlook, assigning a *category* of something like "foreclosures," and then putting enough information in the *notes* field to make searching easy. Every time I do something in regards to that person, I open their file in Outlook and type in notes. I also have a directory called "Foreclosures" and subdirectories with people's names. If a document fits into more than one subdirectory, I file it in all relevant places.

Another system might be as simple as a three-ring binder with tabbed dividers for all your information and some blank pages for spur-of-the-moment notes. Some people work well with labeled file folders, while others prefer shoe boxes.

The point is to set up a system that's comfortable for *you*. If it's not comfortable and designed the way your mind works, then it's useless. Some of my friends have systems that involve nothing more than stacks of paper on the floor. It makes me crazy, but they can always find what they need. Look around you, see the ways you successfully keep track of things, and adapt that system to your foreclosure work.

A procedure is a task. Filling out a form is a procedure. Always corresponding by email and then printing and saving your emails is another one. I'll be giving you lots of procedures in this book. If they need a little adapting to fit into your system, then do it. There's nothing magical about my forms, as long as you obtain the information and do the tasks you need.

Tracking Leads

If your approach to finding properties involves people contacting you, then you'll need some method of keeping track of them. For this, I recommend a ream of three-hole punched paper, eight divider tabs, and a three-ring binder that will stay in your file tub when not in use. Label your tabs as follows:

- Preliminary Review
- Prospects
- Referrers
- Suspects
- Can't Help Now
- Foreclosed
- Avoided Foreclosure
- Other Professionals

If you keep track of your whole life on a computer (like I do), then set up the labels above as categories in Outlook or whatever other address or date software you use. Whatever you use, you must have the ability to enter pretty much unlimited notes in some field, and you must be able to sort by categories.

You'll notice that the tabs do not include one for active properties. That's because, once you've decided that you want to pursue a particular property, you should devote a separate folder to that one.

All papers, notes, and notices relative to that particular property will go in the folder. (More on what goes into the folder comes in later chapters.) If a borrower has more than one property, create more than one file. All of the files can be stored in a plastic container that can sit on your desk, get tossed in the car, or be placed on the kitchen table. It's portable and indestructible—a great combination.

Get into the habit of making notes after you talk to people, and then dropping those notes into the file. Make sure you put a date on your notes. After a few weeks, it gets surprisingly difficult to remember exactly when you obtained certain information. Sometimes it's critically important to know what you knew and when you knew it.

Never throw away any of your papers. You'll want to read through all of them from time to time in order to get a sense of what things work for you and what methods don't work. For example, if you tally your lead sources, you might find that one person sends you tons of leads, but they never turn into anything. Another person sends you very few, but they all ended up in purchases. You might notice that owners of luxury homes either file for Chapter 11 Bankruptcy or sue their lender under some theory, stopping foreclosures. (I'm not saying this is common—it's just an example I made up.) If you see something like this happening time and again, you might decide it's a waste of time to work with upper bracket (luxury) homes.

Meet Jim

In the following pages, you'll meet another workout specialist—Jim. He's fictional, but based on some very real people and their everyday experiences in this industry. Jim will stay with us throughout the book, as he searches for a good property and analyzes which options are best for him.

In order to understand his motivations and restrictions, we need to know a little bit about Jim. He has been out of school for about three years. He has a good job as the assistant manager at an auto parts store. He also has a steady girlfriend he hopes to marry one day. But, there are rumors that Jim's employer might be shutting down several locations and laying off all the employees.

Jim needs an investment that isn't full-time, will grow over the years, and that he can manage on some sort of *touch-it, feel-it* basis, as opposed to stocks and bonds. He also needs something that will not require very much money in a down payment.

He has three foreclosure opportunities. All of them have a first mortgage in default, with a payoff of $85,000.

Property One is three acres of land with a 2,000 square foot building rented out to the United States government on a twenty-five-year lease for use as a post office. The rent is $1,000 per month, but increases each year in order to keep up with inflation. In the trade, we say the building has a "credit tenant," which means a *national* tenant with great credit.

Property Two is virtually identical, but is rented out to a young chiropractor. She has a two-year lease for $1,000 per month. She might have a great credit score, but she's not called a "credit tenant."

Property Three is a modest starter home within walking distance of a good elementary school. It has some *deferred maintenance* (neglected repairs), but it is essentially a sound structure. Jim could either live in it himself or rent it to someone else for about $1,000 per month.

In order to evaluate these properties and make the right choice for which one to buy, Jim needs to:

- engage in some introspection to define his goals and needs;
- learn real estate concepts and analytical tools;
- discover how to evaluate other people's motivations;
- create some checklists for prudent investing; and,
- put it all together to make the right decision.

By the time he's ready to make good buying decisions, you will be, too.

2

Learn to Talk the Talk

I don't want to destroy *my* credibility right off the bat, but I do need to share with you a story from before I got involved in commercial real estate. I was a young lawyer who thought she knew everything. To be honest, I was *convinced* I knew everything. My husband, Bill, had been making his living in commercial real estate for many years, and was trying to share with me some of the knowledge he'd accumulated. He concentrated on sophisticated principles, but didn't realize I was incredibly ignorant about basic concepts.

One day, we were out driving around, looking at houses, and we passed a small shopping center. One wall had collapsed, and the parking lot contained huge sinkholes. There were no tenants. Otherwise, it looked brand-new.

Bill pointed, and told me, "It's tied up in litigation among the owner, the bank, the contractor, and the engineer. They'd just finished construction when the first sinkhole appeared, so there's never been a single tenant in the strip center. That's why…"

The part after "That's why" was supposed to be my lesson for the day—what a prudent investor should have done differently. I never heard that little nugget of wisdom. I stopped listening when he told me it was a strip center.

I'd never heard of such a thing. In my entire life, I'd never even dreamed there were shopping centers devoted to strip joints. The other tenants probably sold porn and heaven only knew what else. Bill kept rattling on, speaking commercial real estate, while my ears kept hearing the everyday meaning.

Finally, he figured out that I'd completely missed the boat on the strip center issue. He explained that a *strip center* was a small shopping center, usually laid out in a rectangular *strip*, with every tenant having a separate entrance. The experience taught me a valuable lesson. Whenever you're sharing knowledge with someone who is not steeped in your field, start out with a few basics regarding concepts and lingo.

There are lots of reasons this is important. Someone might try to tell you something really important, but you might ignore him or her because you don't understand the significance. Lenders, investors, and people who can give you leads might think you're a lightweight because you don't use the vocabulary of your profession. With an understanding of the vocabulary and the concepts, if you are faced with something that wasn't covered in this book, it won't stump you.

Instant Credibility

For some instant credibility and to compete effectively with much more experienced real estate investors, it's important to remember two things.

1. Property owners facing foreclosure will do business with the person who *seems* most likely to solve their problems.
2. Bankers loaning money will do business with the person who *seems* most likely to repay the loan **and** who *seems* most likely to borrow more money in the future from that same bank.

Insight:
Banking is a competitive, cutthroat business, and a one-shot customer is less valuable than an investor. Like other people, bankers never have enough time to return all phone calls, answer all letters, or meet with everyone. Some people get ignored. Knowing the proper lingo will help make sure you're the person who gets his or her phone calls returned.

Some of the following terms will involve concepts important to buying foreclosure properties. Others are general real estate terms that might come up in a conversation. Once people find out you're involved in real estate, they'll turn to you with all sorts of questions—you want to be ready.

Income Stream

The most important concept in real estate investing is *income stream*. I like to think of this as the river of money coming out of a property. Knowledgeable people talk about the *size* and the *strength* of the income stream. Strength pertains to reliability. Of the properties Jim is examining, the income stream *seems* to be identical for all three. On the other hand, the one from the post office is the most reliable. It's the strongest income stream. It makes the post office the most valuable property—at least on the surface.

What's important to know at this point is that most people who try to buy foreclosure properties are investors. The larger and stronger the income stream from a property, the more competition you're going to have from other buyers. Conversely, the smaller and less reliable the income stream, the more opportunities you have to make a deal at a reasonable price.

Land

Raw land, or land with no income-producing improvements, doesn't have an income stream coming out of it. Some people think raw land means there's nothing built on it. That's not completely true. A thousand-acre peach orchard has nothing built on it, but it's not raw law. The property produces income every year. Because it's designed to generate an income stream, it's not raw land.

If you evaluate an investment based on its income stream, then raw land doesn't add very much to your analysis. It has *potential,* but that's not the same thing as *income.* When a banker loans money against raw land, he usually loans a smaller amount—maybe 50% of the value instead of 80% of the value.

Also, appraisers are usually more conservative in evaluating raw land than improved land, so the loan value might be relatively low.

This is important because sometimes foreclosure properties are a mixture of raw and improved land. Jim's post office sits on three acres of land. It probably needs all that space for the building, a parking lot, driveways, outside mailboxes, and delivery vehicles. The appraiser who evaluated the post office for a loan looked only at the income stream in order to come up with an appraised value. This method is fairly easy and reliable. You can do the same thing. Chapter 12 explains exactly how appraisals are done, so you can duplicate them yourself. There's little risk in buying this type of property. There's also lots of competition for that reason.

The chiropractor probably needs just the ¼ acre occupied by her building and four parking places. The remaining 2¾ acres is called *surplus land* or *excess land*. The value of this property, and how much you can borrow to buy it, depends on how you describe it to a banker. If Jim wants to leave the chiropractor in place and simply collect your rent every month, then the value is based *only* on the income stream.

If, on the other hand, Jim plans to build more offices and rent them out to podiatrists and optometrists, then suddenly the surplus land has a value separate and in addition to the income stream. The chiropractor's office might require a little more imagination than the post office, but could turn out to be the far better purchase. There's development potential, the appraisal will end up being higher, and Jim will be able to borrow more money. In fact, in some instances a person can borrow 100% of the purchase price plus additional development money if he or she has a credible plan to increase the income from a piece of property.

If you're buying property without a current or reasonably predictable future income stream, then any banker must look at your personal income for the source of funds to make mortgage payments. Once you've reached your "loan limit," you can't borrow any more money. However, always remember that every piece of income-producing property stands on its own two feet. You won't use up your personal credit as each property has its own *credit limit*.

> **Insight:**
> Most multi-million dollar loans on income-producing property don't even require a personal guarantee from the borrower. The loan is so huge and so far beyond the individual's credit limit that the lender doesn't waste its time obtaining a guarantee or evaluating the borrower's individual credit. Sometimes it's easier to borrow millions of dollars on income-producing property than $35,000 to buy a car.

Due Diligence

Another critically important real estate concept is *due diligence*. This means, generally, doing all the things you need to do *before the fact* to satisfy yourself that you're making a good, relatively safe purchase.

The steps included in due diligence will change from property to property. Before you can pick out the right items, or even know how to approach investing in foreclosures, you need to know about different types of property.

Property Types

The following discussion of property types isn't comprehensive. Some categories will overlap, but it will give you an idea for starting places. I recommend you specialize in a particular type of property and learn it thoroughly before you branch out. That way, you get to master a specialized subject instead of having to learn a lot of new stuff with every single real estate purchase.

Troubled property, or sometimes *distressed property*, is a polite way bankers and investors talk about a borrower who can't or won't make his or her mortgage payments on time. The term has nothing to do with the property itself.

Residential

Most investors start with *single-family residential*. It's generally used to describe a house, but could include a condominium. Smart buyers will usually limit themselves to a particular price range. Finding tenants or buyers for a $50,000 house is entirely different from finding them for a $500,000 house. Fixing up the more modest home can generally be done yourself, while the larger one will require hired professionals. The profit on an expensive house should be larger, but the risk is usually proportionately greater.

Single-family residential properties are typically *owner/occupied*, meaning the owner lives there. Sometimes they're investment properties, used for rental income. Knowing this makes a difference in how you evaluate whether you want to buy the property. Some investors specialize in owner/occupied foreclosures because they think it provides a ready-made tenant when the former owner wants to stay and pay rent. Other people avoid them like the plague. They think single-family residential is too much work, and owner/occupied presents too much risk of something going wrong at the last minute. There's no wrong answer here.

A *condominium* is a type of single-family residential property. What makes it special is that it's an ownership arrangement in which each person owns a particular area, and the condominium association owns all the common areas, such as hallways, elevators, sidewalks, and lawns. Condominiums generally have strict rules, and owners are responsible for their proportionate share of some potentially expensive repairs, or for improvements like new roofs and landscaping. As a result, buying a condo in foreclosure requires additional homework on your part.

Multi-family residential property could be a duplex (two units in one building), a fourplex (four apartments—usually two upstairs and two downstairs), a sixplex, or something larger, which is called, simply, an apartment building or apartment complex. Even if all you own is one duplex, and you live in one side of it, you can legitimately tell people, *I invest in multi-family residential properties.*

If, on the other hand, you own 250 houses that you rent out, these are all single-family residential *properties*, even though you, personally, rent to multiple *families*. You invest in single-family residential properties.

Commercial

Commercial property is typically an office, retail space, a sit-down restaurant, or a fast food establishment. Except in small towns, people further specialize within commercial property. I, for example, know all the office buildings in my part of town—about six million square feet of office space. I know what the market rents are, whose leases are expiring, and who's coming to town and looking for space. I know how much it costs to build an office building, and what rents someone would have to charge in order to justify new construction. I could confidently invest in a small office building, but would be lost trying to figure out what to do with a restaurant site.

Retail

Retail further breaks down into single- or multi-tenant buildings, convenience stores, strip centers, anchored and nonanchored shopping centers, regional malls, lifestyle centers, and big boxes. Most investors specialize within a price range rather than retail category.

The C-Store Shelter

Professionals call a convenience store a *C-store*. These are very desirable investments because you can get bigger tax deductions than for other properties. If you find an opportunity to buy a convenience store before foreclosure, you can probably find all sorts of partners to help with the money for the investment.

Here's why. The IRS allows you to write off a portion of the purchase price of your property every year. It's kind of a game everyone's agreed to play. The premise of the game is this: dirt never gets less valuable over the years, but anything on top of the dirt declines in value the older it gets. This could be buildings, roads, fences, light poles, or peach trees. The IRS has rules for how long it takes different things to eventually wear out and become completely worthless. Sometimes they really do wear out in that time period; sometimes it takes longer; and, sometimes it happens much more quickly. It doesn't matter—this IRS game bears no relationship to reality. It's just a system that everyone has agreed to *pretend* is real.

The process of wearing out is called *depreciation*. It's a deductible expense on your taxes. Depreciation lets you write off large expenses for real estate, even though you don't have to write checks for those expenses. That's called *sheltering income* because other income (such as from your job) can *hide* under the shelter of the depreciation tax deductions and not be taxed by the IRS. High-income professionals, like doctors and lawyers, are always looking for ways to shelter income. That's why they make logical partners if you need someone to put up the cash while you contribute the time and know-how to buy foreclosure properties.

The ability to write off depreciation deductions is one of the major advantages of investing in real estate instead of other things. Because of that, it's critically important to understand. The central concept to depreciation deductions is knowing the IRS's opinion about the *useful life* of different kinds of property. Useful life is an estimate of how long something will last before it becomes completely worthless. The IRS does not care that a rental house worth $50,000 in 1976 might be worth $150,000 in 2005. You are allowed to *pretend* it will be worthless in 2005, and to write off depreciation every year until 2005.

According to the IRS, most commercial buildings will decline evenly in value over the course of 39 years and then be worthless at the end. They are also of the opinion that residential properties will last only 27.5 years. For some odd reason, the IRS has decided that convenience stores will last only 15 years. So, you can write off $1/15^{th}$ of their value every year. That means you can *shelter* over twice as much income with a C-store as you can with a dry cleaners occupying the exact same building at the exact same spot. That's what makes them such hot investments. Doctors, lawyers, and other high-income people love to invest in convenience stores. You'll be able to find lots of partners if you run across such an opportunity.

Shopping Center

A typical *strip center* has five to ten tenants on a single story with parking out front. Each tenant usually has a small space—around 1,000 square feet.

In shopping centers (strip centers and malls), *anchor* refers to a big tenant that attracts customers, who will then also visit the smaller tenants. An anchor might be a grocery store, a department store, or a decorating center. It anchors and holds steady the constant stream of visitors. Because anchors are so important to the well-being of the other tenants, many anchor leases will prohibit the anchor tenant from closing during the term of its lease. In the trade, we say the lease has a prohibition against *going dark*. In other words, even if the anchor were willing to turn out the lights, move to another part of town, but continue paying rent at the old location, it wouldn't be allowed. That's because, if the anchor closes, the traffic flow to the shopping center dries up and the smaller tenants eventually go out of business, too.

If someone tells you about a shopping center opportunity, you can start your due diligence right away and ask two questions, "Who's the anchor?" and, "Is there a prohibition against going dark?" These questions, all by themselves, let people know you're an intelligent investor.

> **Insight:**
> Sometimes asking the right questions gives you more credibility than knowing the right answers. Questions mark you as curious or cautious; unsolicited speeches about real estate principles mark you as a bore.

Regional malls are the huge, multi-department store centers with access via interior corridors lined by other stores. They're not as popular as they once were. That means you're going to see more prospects to buy these out of foreclosure. They can present fabulous opportunities if you're energetic and creative. People are buying them cheaply and turning them into antique malls, training centers, city halls, medical complexes, and megachurches.

The newer *lifestyle malls* are all the rage in temperate climates like California and the South. People park in front of each store and walk or take trams between stores. There's generally artwork, entertainment, multiple specialty restaurants, and other amenities to attract people and encourage them to linger. Think of a lifestyle mall as being the suburban equivalent of 5th Avenue in New York City or Rodeo Drive in Los Angeles. I doubt you'll be in a position to buy one of these, but it's always nice to be able to fling around the right terminology when talking to friends at a picnic. You never know where your prospects might come from, and credibility is critically important for getting leads on properties.

Big Box

A *big box* is a large, plain vanilla building suitable for a Wal-Mart, Target, or something similar. *Vanilla* is another real estate investor's term, meaning "easily changeable into anything." Many big boxes formerly occupied by K-Mart or Sears are being converted to climate-controlled self-storage, fitness centers, or craft malls.

The opposite of a vanilla building is a *purpose-built building*. A bank, a car dealership, or a widget factory are all built in a specialized way for a particular purpose. It's hard to adapt them for something different. You need to think about that when looking at a foreclosure. The greater the variety of things you can do with a property after you buy it, the less your risk is going to be.

Industrial

Industrial properties are usually manufacturing, assemblage (putting together components manufactured some place else), high tech, or warehouses. Most people tend to think of these as high-risk investments to buy out of foreclosure, but that's not always the case. A great industrial property, with a terrific tenant who always pays the rent on time, might be in foreclosure because the landlord takes all the money from that property in order to pay *other* bills. Or, the owner might have given a mortgage on that property as additional security on another site that was in trouble and unable to pay its bills. (This is called *cross collateralization*.) As a result, the lender is foreclosing on one troubled property with a bad tenant or no tenant, *and* on a good property that's a terrific investment. You don't have to buy both of them at the foreclosure— you can buy just the good property.

Flipping

Many people attracted to investing in real estate want to buy today, literally sell tomorrow, and make a killing during their twenty-four hours of ownership. It is called *flipping*. These practitioners are the day-traders of real estate. The game is fast-paced, potentially lucrative, and certainly dangerous.

Foreclosure Flippings

Other foreclosure books advocate a type of flipping in which you obligate the borrower under a contract, leave yourself lots of back doors, and then try to sell the *contract* to someone else. It is risk free because *you* have no obligations. I don't recommend it for two reasons. First, it's not fair to the borrower, who has a false sense of security that you're going to buy this property. Most borrowers don't understand that if you can't execute the flip, you aren't going to close. Second, you have to practically steal the property in order for you, and the other investor, to both make money. That's not the message of this book, and I don't think you'll feel comfortable doing business in that way.

In order for you, and the person who buys the contract, to both make a profit, you have to lock in a purchase at a bargain-basement price. Two people making an acceptable profit requires a much greater *spread* between purchase price and sale price. Plus since you might not find a buyer, you have to build *back doors* into your purchase contract so you can slip out easily without any obligation to buy. This isn't fair to the seller—he or she thinks someone's honestly working on a purchase, but you're not.

Even with full disclosure, it's still not fair. In order to do a flip, you have to tie up the seller under a contract, so he or she can't do anything else, while *you* have all the flexibility in the world to find a buyer.

The better practice, if you can't buy a property yourself, is to refer the borrower to someone else. In the alternative, form relationships with people who have money, but little time, and who want to invest in real estate. Establish your purchase requirements early in your relationship, and then go out and find foreclosure properties. It has the same practical effect as a flip—you get in for no money down and secure a fairly immediate profit—but it leaves none of the dashed expectations and emotional wreckage behind.

Outside of the specialized foreclosure-purchase world, *flipping* means buying properties and then holding them for relatively short periods of time. During times of rapidly escalating real estate prices, people will often buy real estate, hold it for sixty or ninety days, and then sell it for tens or hundreds of thousands dollars more than they paid. There's nothing morally or ethically wrong, but it is speculation and gambling, pure and simple.

3

Buy a Property for Your Personal Residence

Many of you will use this book to help you buy a home in which to live. This might seem like the easiest property to buy, but it's really one of the most difficult. The top three reasons for this are as follows.

1. Buying a home is an emotional decision, as well as a practical one. You can do all the financial and neighborhood analysis I recommend, but you still have to add in some soft points such as architectural style, proximity to relatives, neighborhood personality, and whether or not you can live with harvest gold appliances until you can afford to buy new ones.

2. With a home, you tend to live with bad decisions longer because it's such a pain to pack up and move again. It makes you a lot more cautious. Whereas with an investment property, you are not living there, so it is easier to sell it to someone else and get on with life.

3. Your range of acceptable properties is smaller with a home. You need the right school system, the best resale value, amenities such as day care, and grocery stores, plus an evaluation of how long your daily commute is going to be. With investment property, if the numbers make sense, you pretty much don't care about anything else—so you have more choices.

> **Insight:**
> This leads to Rule Number One of investing—
> *You Can't Fall in Love with a Deal.*

I didn't invent Rule Number One. Investors say it all the time. It means you have to analyze the property in a clear-headed, by-the-numbers kind of way without getting emotional and overlooking problems. To me, that's pretty easy. I just use my forms, plug in the information I need, and out pops an answer at the end about whether this is a prudent investment or not. Homes are harder because, of course, you're *supposed* to fall in love with the place.

Evaluate What You Want

Before I tell you how to find, evaluate, and buy properties, you need to decide what *you* want to buy. I designed the following form primarily for homeowners, but it should also be used if you want to invest in residential properties. The questions will help you pinpoint your areas of interest. This is critically important because, otherwise, you waste a lot of time looking at things that aren't right for you.

Worse than wasting your own time, you're wasting the time and hopes of someone who's facing foreclosure. It's not ethical to *practice* on people who have every right to believe you might be able to help them. You're dealing with real people here; this isn't some abstract exercise. Be sensitive, be fair, and do your homework *before* you start getting someone's hopes up.

To help focus, fill out the questionnaire and decide how you want to proceed. It is for homebuyers, or for people who want to invest in single-family residential properties. It's a type of property that is easy to pinpoint for likes and dislikes. As I said earlier, investment properties are usually just a numbers game.

What kind of home do you want to buy?			
	Perfect	Okay	Sudden Death
# of bedrooms			
# of bathrooms			
Square footage			
Brick/wood/etc.*			
Lot size			
Landscaping			
Age of house*			
School system			
Daily commute time			
Close/far neighbors*			
Good shape or fixer-upper			
Distance to fire station/hydrant*			
Features (pool, etc.)			
Other features			
Cable television available			
High speed internet available			
Average age of neighbors			
Price range			

The items with an asterisk (*) also affect your insurance premiums. If you're a first-time homebuyer, talk to your insurance agent before shopping.

Add your own items and make this chart as long or as short as you want. The important thing is to focus on your particular *wants* and *needs* so you don't waste your time, or someone else's hopes on things that just aren't going to work out.

Screen Your Choices

Next, I'm going to show you a system to help you be as efficient as possible in finding the right property for you. If you have to go through a lengthy process to look at every residential foreclosure property you learn about, then you're going to get burned out pretty quickly. What you need to do, first and fast, is weed out the unacceptable ones.

I suggest you duplicate the chart on page 25, with extra lines for the additional features that are important to you or that represent sudden death. At the top of the sheet, above the table, type in something similar to the following:

Property Address: _____

Date Learned about Property: _____

How Learned about Property: _____

Date Obtained Initial Info. about Property:_____

Name and Phone # of Informant:_____

(At the bottom of the sheet, leave a space for "Additional Thoughts/Info.")

Now, make about twenty copies. Put them in a three-ring binder so, as you complete them on different properties, you can flip through quickly and easily. The reason you want to do this (and keep those sheets even if you reject a property) is because sometimes patterns will develop as you review your sheets. You'll start recognizing that a certain referrer always tells you about properties with sudden death features, for example. You don't want to drop that person from your Christmas card list, but you probably don't want to invest a lot of time taking them out to lunch, either.

The purpose of the form is to allow you to *screen* or *prequalify* properties, just like a lender will prequalify you. When you learn about a property, pull out a clean form. Fill in the relevant information about address, etc. When you're able to talk to someone with knowledge about the details of the property, *the very first questions you ask will be the sudden death questions.*

There's no point in listening to the homeowner gush over the gourmet kitchen, Olympic pool, five bedrooms with hand-painted murals on the walls, and the really cheap price, if it's a wood frame house and you're passionate about brick. This is a sudden death property. Hearing *first* about all the wonderful stuff makes you want to stretch and work to overcome the things that are bad for you. (*Hmmm*, you'll think, *Maybe I can buy this house and then, in a few years, brick it up...*)

You're going to have to do a lot of work to buy the right foreclosure property, but the rewards will be great. In order to be able to invest, you have to be efficient. That's why you ask the sudden death questions first.

Determine if You Can Afford It

You also need to decide how much home you can afford. Besides saving you a lot of time by not looking at things that aren't economically feasible, it will also make it easier to negotiate fairly and ethically with borrowers. First, you don't want to give false hope to someone facing foreclosure, and then only late in the game find out you can't buy his or her property. In addition, you can also evaluate how much leeway you have in paying a higher price or giving back a second mortgage to the borrower.

The following table will help you calculate monthly mortgage payments. This doesn't include escrows for taxes and insurance.

Each $1,000 of borrowed money will cost you the following monthly payments. (Approximates, because of rounding)		
Interest Rate:	20-Year Mortgage	30-Year Mortgage
6%	$7.16	$6.00
6¼%	$7.31	$6.16
6½%	$7.46	$6.32
6¾%	$7.60	$6.49
7%	$7.75	$6.65
7¼%	$7.90	$6.82
7½%	$8.06	$6.99
7¾%	$8.21	$7.16
8%	$8.36	$7.34
8¼%	$8.52	$7.51
8½%	$8.68	$7.69

If interest rates are at 6%, and you can afford monthly mortgage payments of $700, then here's your calculation.

1. According to the table, 6% interest on a 30-year mortgage means that every $1,000 of borrowed money costs $6 per month.
2. You can afford $700 per month. By dividing $700 by $6, it results in 116 (more or less).
3. If each $6 payment means $1,000 in borrowed money, then 116 payments of $6 would be the same thing as 116 loans of $1,000 each, or $116,000 in borrowed money.

Here's the shorthand version:

Monthly payment you can afford:	(a) _____
Monthly cost of $1,000 loan:	(b) _____
Divide (a) by (b):	(c) _____
Multiply (c) by $1,000:	(d) _____

The answer, (d), is how much mortgage you can afford.

Example: Suppose interest rates are at 6% and you find a property worth $120,000 that can be purchased for the $95,000 mortgage balance, but the homeowner wants an extra $5,000 for his equity. Most foreclosure buyers would tell the homeowner to go fly a kite, because they're going to lose the property and their equity anyway. You're different because you want to be fair and ethical, *and* because you'll have the analytical tools that will allow you to be fair and ethical.

Using the table and the formula, an extra $5,000 at 6% interest on a 30-year term will cost you an additional $29.98 per month. Can you afford that? If so, do it! The small amount of additional expense each month will be forgotten fairly quickly, but you'll not risk losing a good deal, and the former owner will preserve his dignity and have a little cash to start over. Once you know how to analyze a potential purchase, you have the freedom to be generous and flexible, because you'll know the real costs involved and need not fear them.

When calculating how much home you can afford, don't forget to include insurance, property taxes, maintenance, and other such items. Remember that your commute to work might be longer, resulting in higher gas expenses and increased auto insurance premiums.

The Tax Breaks

You'll hear from many sources that you can afford a higher mortgage payment than rent payment because of the tax savings. It's certainly true that the interest portion of your mortgage payment is deductible every year. At least in the first couple of years, almost all of your mortgage payment will be interest. If you're in the 15% tax bracket, then every $100 you earn above a certain base amount will cost you $15 in federal income taxes. Logically, then, a $100 mortgage interest deduction will save you $15 in taxes.

My advice is, if you're in the 15% tax bracket, don't count on tax deductions saving you enough money to compensate for a mortgage payment higher than you think you can afford. Even if it's not things like repairs or a lawnmower, then it's going to be a swing set for the children, new curtains in the living room, a few shelves in the garage, and other things you never thought about when you rented.

Insight:
Almost always, unforeseen property expenses will add 10% or 15% to your annual budget.

For higher tax brackets, the interest deduction can be significant, but there is a trap to consider. Not all of your income is taxed at the higher percentage. Some amount is tax free, some is taxed at 10%, some at 15%, some at 25%, and so on. Here's an example of the fallacy that misleads so many people.

Suppose I'm single and earn $35,000 per year. That puts me in the 25% tax bracket. Most of my mortgage payments will be interest in the first year, so most will be deductible. I think to myself, "If I can afford $750 a month in rent payments, then I can afford $1,000 a month in mortgage payments because of my 25% tax bracket." I rationalize that the $1,000 mortgage interest deduction will shelter $1,000 of income on which I'd otherwise have to pay $250 in taxes.

The way this actually works is a little more complicated. Under current (2005) tax laws, the first $7,150 of income, for a single filer, has no taxes. The next $21,900 is taxed at 15%, and the final $5,950 is taxed at 25%. When you do the calculations, a mortgage payment of $1,000 a month, *even assuming the entire payment is deductible interest*, will save you only $200 per month—not $250.

To figure out your own tax savings, you can go on the Internet and search for a mortgage calculator and tax savings calculator. (Hundreds of financial websites have them.) Or, ask a mortgage broker who's interested in gaining your business. People who are really intent on being self-sufficient can get the tax tables from the IRS, a mortgage loan calculator from an office supply store, and use the following formula:

Adjusted Gross Income before mortgage deductions:	(a) _____
Tax on Adjusted Gross Income (AGI):	(b) _____
AGI after you subtract first year's mortgage interest:	(c) _____
Tax on new AGI:	(d) _____
Subtract (d) from (b):	(e) _____
Divide (e) by 12:	(f) _____

The answer, (f), is how much you'll save each month because of the mortgage interest deduction.

• • • • •

Now that you know what you want, both in terms of amenities and size of monthly payment, you're ready to start looking for the perfect home. Don't skip the next chapter, "Deciding What You Want in Investment Property," because sometimes a house you see as your future home is simply an investment from the perspective of the current owner. In order to negotiate effectively with that person, you need to understand his or her viewpoint, and how he or she analyzes the investment.

4

Decide What You Want in Investment Property

If you're reading this book so you can invest in properties, you need to start with a different sort of analysis, and *then* proceed to some variant of the homeowner form from Chapter 3. The following questions will help you pinpoint the opportunities that are right for you.

Do you want to immediately supplement your income?

If you answer "yes," then it indicates you can't afford to buy a property that will have negative cash flow. *Negative cash flow* means, in order to pay the mortgage and other bills every month, you'll have to add some of your personal money to the amount coming in from the property. If you need to immediately *supplement* your income, then I'm assuming you can't afford to make *less* money each month. You're also *risk intolerant*. It's a fancy way of saying you can't afford to gamble on a property—it has to be pretty much 100% certain of cash flowing. As we work through the investment exercises for properties, later, you want to ignore anything that does not have a 95% probability of generating a positive cash flow.

Many people will tell you a property has a negative cash flow, at a particular purchase price, but still makes sense because of the money you'll save on your taxes. The implication is that the money you save on taxes will be *more* than the negative cash flow on the property. *This almost never works out to be true!* It's an entirely different calculation than the one I showed you for home mortgage interest deductions. Refer to Chapter 13—Rental Properties and Cash Flow—for the formulas. You should buy an investment property because it makes economic sense, all by itself. Tax considerations are a bonus.

Do you want to concentrate on building future income?

You may be planning for things like college expenses and retirement, but can afford some negative cash flow or breakeven right now. If so, then you probably want something you can buy now and hold for many years. It will be important for you to find a residential property in a stable neighborhood, or a commercial property that is *very* unlikely to decline in value over time.

If the property declines in value, then your rents will decrease, also. You want your rents to increase, the mortgage payments to remain the same, and your cash flow to increase as a result.

Property values are affected by changing neighborhoods (office into industrial, residential into small retail, for example) and by something called *deferred maintenance*. Maintenance, as you know, is what you do to maintain a property—repairing the gutters, replacing damaged siding, painting, and other things. Deferred maintenance means you've been putting it off, deferring it, possibly for years and years. Most of us would say that a property is *run down*, but investors don't use such a common expression.

Insight:

If you want future income, then you need a stable area and a property with minimal maintenance needs. Remember, that really adorable Victorian house built in 1890 is high maintenance! The boring brick ranch with tile floors and area rugs is low maintenance. Buy the Victorian to fix up and sell. Buy the ranch to keep forever and rent out.

Do you want the equivalent of a savings account?

Perhaps you want a safe property that can break even each year without generating cash flow, but you want it to *appreciate* (grow in value) so you can sell it for a huge profit sometime in the distant future. If you don't need immediate income and want to avoid any risk, then you want the same properties as the ones identified in the previous section. If you can afford *some* risk, then you can probably also buy properties that *might* make a larger profit when you sell them, later.

As a general rule, risk is related to how many properties you have, and what your other financial resources are. Let's look at a four-bedroom brick house within two blocks of the elementary school in a neighborhood of $150,000 homes. You can buy it for $50,000. Is it a good deal? If this is your first investment, you might conduct all your due diligence, not find anything wrong, and *still* decide that this deal is too good to be true. You might pass on it, because you are risk-intolerant.

There could be something wrong that wouldn't show up on an inspection report. I bought a terrific foreclosure house in an exclusive neighborhood, but the former owner was supposed to have been a drug dealer. People were afraid of the house. I felt I could deal with that problem, so I got a bargain.

If you own multiple properties, you might want to gamble on a risky one because you can afford to get hurt if it turns out badly, but you stand to make a lot of money if it turns out well. Just remember Rule Two of Investing—

If you can't afford to gamble, don't gamble!

Do you want to buy and sell properties fairly rapidly?

Four types of people want to buy and sell properties fairly rapidly.

1. Investors who like to make enough money to live on for a year, but who don't want to work for an entire year.

35

2. Investors who like to make periodic chunks of money for life's extras, such as a new bass boat or a two-week Caribbean cruise.

3. Homeowners who want to take advantage of tax laws that let them sell their principal residence once every two years and not pay any income taxes.

4. People who just don't have the desire to engage in long-term relationships with tenants. (Remember, your time is worth something, too. If you're unlucky enough to have high maintenance tenants, you might make more money, for your time, working at McDonald's.)

With a buy-and-sell-often strategy, you have to make a larger profit in order to cover your acquisition and sale expenses. You can do it through buying at terrific bargains, or through buying fixer-uppers.

It's fairly simple to set your investment parameters. You decide how much profit you have to make in order to justify your time and efforts, and then you don't pursue anything unless it meets those criteria.

Put the Tools in Practice

To illustrate the principles discussed, I'm going to work through Jim's decision-making process as he looks at his three different foreclosure opportunities. It will give you a good idea of how to adapt the tools in this chapter for your own situation.

Jim is a young man who wants to get married. In order to do that, he feels that he needs some financial stability, just in case he loses his job. The prospect of being unemployed is currently very real, because his company is shutting down stores in many states. On the other hand, he's employed today, knows his job is secure for at least one year, has a good credit score, and owns his home.

This is what Jim's thought process should be in deciding what kind of property to buy.

- ◆ I need stability and certainty for my future family.
- ◆ I can't afford very much risk.
- ◆ I'm not a people-person and probably won't have any patience with tenants.
- ◆ A family needs a home, so I shouldn't do anything that puts my home in danger, such as take out a home equity loan in order to fund my real estate purchases.
- ◆ I know my job is safe for at least one year. As a result, any property I buy can have negative cash flow for the first year, but has to have positive cash flow after that.
- ◆ If I lose my job as an assistant manager, I still want to find work doing the same thing. I might be unemployed for as long as one year. If I cut out all unnecessary expenses, my future wife and I can live on $1,000 per month. On the other hand, I don't need a property that will completely support me from now on, because I do plan on getting a paycheck and health insurance again.

At this point in his life, Jim needs a low-risk property (or two or three) that can have a negative cash flow and take up all his spare time in the first year. Jim, and the important people in his life, can tolerate a complete lack of free time as long as they know, up front, what the duration is going to be. If they agree that the time commitment is worth the reward, and is finite, then Jim can proceed without any guilt.

Because Jim is willing to give up one year of his life, if need be, but not more, he needs to think about what happens in the second year of ownership. If he plans to keep the property, then it should be able to support the expenses of a management company and still have a cash flow of at least $1,000 per month starting in Year Two. He's willing to hire a management company, and incur the 6% to 10% additional fee it will cost, because he's unwilling to assume to responsibilities of self-managing his property.

Jim's not limited to being a landlord, though. He might want a property that he can buy cheaply, fix up, and then sell within twelve to thirteen months for at least a $12,000 profit *after taxes*. That's because he's calculated that he might need $1,000 per month for twelve months in order to meet living expenses while he's unemployed. It's all right to earn it all at once and put it in the bank. The reason he wants to make the sale sometime twelve to thirteen months after purchase is because he must hold a property more than twelve months to qualify for low capital gains tax rates.

At first blush, here's what the three properties mean in Jim's situation.

Post Office

The Post Office offers low risk, low need for tenant hand-holding, and moderate need for property management. Probably all the maintenance is the landlord's responsibility because the US government just isn't set up to call a glazier every time a hailstorm breaks a window. Good, steady income, but no opportunity to make a huge immediate profit because there will be lots of competition from other investors to buy this property. Jim won't be able to buy this property at much of a bargain.

Chiropractor

The chiropractor building is somewhat higher risk, but still probably has a low need for management because professionals like to stay in the same offices unless they outgrow them. Probably all maintenance is the tenant's responsibility, but this varies depending on the lease. This property presents the opportunity to develop the surplus land or to sell it off to someone else for development. As a result, it can provide regular income *and* quick profits.

Starter Home

Risk depends on an evaluation of whether the former owner wants to rent the house or whether Jim wants to sell or rent his own house and move into the foreclosure home. Residential tenants almost always require more management than commercial ones. That's because residential leases usually leave all repairs and upkeep to the landlord, and because it's just good business to maintain a personal relationship with your tenants. If the landlord is just a P.O. Box where the rent checks are sent, then the tenant has no loyalty to the landlord. Tenants will move out more often and they'll not be as careful about keeping the property in good shape. They'll still call you to make needed repairs, but they might not ask permission before painting the bedroom walls black.

Jim's Initial Analysis

At this point, Jim is probably leaning towards the property with the chiropractor as a tenant. It fulfills many of his immediate needs. In addition, Jim might want to open his own accounting practice some day, and could use the property for his own offices.

After you've worked through a similar analysis for your needs, use the table on the following page to help bring them into sharper focus.

Requirements Necessary For Any Investment Property

Put an "X" in one box for each question.

Will you need:	Strongly Agree	Agree	Neutral	Disagree	Strongly Disagree
No money down					
Minimal money down					
Financing despite bad credit					
Immediate cash flow					
Cash flow within one year					
Appreciation over time					
Fast sale and profit					
Large, fast sale and profit					
Management by self					
Maintain/repair by self					
Minimal self-management					
Minimal risk					
Total "x"s in each column:					

If Jim completes the table, his would look like the one on the following page.

Jim's requirements for any investment property he wishes to buy.

Will you need:	Strongly Agree	Agree	Neutral	Disagree	Strongly Disagree
No money down		X			
Minimal money down		X			
Financing despite bad credit					X
Immediate cash flow				X	
Cash flow within one year	X				
Appreciation over time			X		
Fast sale and profit				X	
Large, fast sale and profit				X	
Management by self					X
Maintain/repair by self					X
Minimal self-management	X				
Minimal risk	X				
Total "x"s in each column:	3	2	1	3	3

Jim has a small savings account, so he doesn't *need* little or no money down, but he wouldn't be offended by the opportunity, so he's neutral on those issues. He has great credit. He doesn't need immediate cash flow, because he has a good job. But his whole reason for investing is that he may need cash flow within a year in order to support his family.

Jim may decide to keep his investment for the long term, as a sort of savings account, or he may decide to sell it as soon as he's confident of good job security. As a result, he says he's neutral about long-term appreciation. He also says he "disagrees" regarding the need for quick appreciation and sale, but his next three answers indicate that he doesn't have much tolerance for managing or maintaining it himself.

The chart focuses Jim on the fact that he's not cut out to be a landlord unless he can leave the management, leasing, and maintenance to other people. That's okay, but it increases his expenses each month. If they're more than Jim can afford, then he might need to concentrate on buying and selling properties at a profit in order to build up a nest egg in case he becomes unemployed.

The Bottom Line

Nothing is 100%, but there are some general rules of thumb about different types of investment properties. They include the following.

- In single-family residential, it's easier to sell a property to another investor if you have a good tenant in place with at least eight months left on their lease.
- On the other hand, you can usually sell that same property for a higher price to someone who wants to live in it. An owner who wants to live in or use their property is called an "owner/occupier."
- Single-family residential rental property is usually a good starting place for new investors because the risk is relatively small and the leasing, maintenance, and management problems can be handled by yourself, thereby minimizing expenses.
- Multi-family residential rental property is easier to manage than the same number of units in single-family units, because everything is together in the same place.

◆ Multi-family properties will usually give you a larger return per unit than single-family properties, if you self-manage. You can buy four houses for $60,000 each (a total of $240,000) and rent them out for $550 per month, which gives you a decent return on your investment. Or, you can buy a fourplex for $200,000 ($50,000 per unit), rent each unit out for $550 per month, and get an even better return on your money.

◆ With a multi-family building, it's easier to hire a management company to do the leasing, collect rents, and periodically inspect the units to make sure the tenants aren't destroying them.

◆ Commercial property has a lower turnover in tenants because the leases are usually for three, five, or ten years.

◆ In commercial property, many times you can shift all of the ownership expenses, such as taxes, insurance, and maintenance, to the tenant. These are called *triple net leases*. *Net* means what's left after paying expenses. *Triple net* means that the trio of ordinary expenses—taxes, insurance, and maintenance—don't have to be paid out of the rent money the landlord receives every month. The tenant pays those expenses, in addition to rent. If someone tells you that two office buildings each rent for $1,000 per month, you need to know if that rent is gross or net. *Gross* means the owner pays the expenses. *Net* means the tenant pays some or all of the expenses. It makes a difference in how you evaluate which property to buy.

◆ Commercial properties take longer to lease if they're vacant, so they are generally riskier than residential properties.

◆ Just like residential properties, a commercial owner/occupier, or someone who wants to buy the property to use him- or herself rather than rent it out, will generally pay a higher price than an investor who wants a tenant. That's because of Rule Number One of Investing—"You can't fall in love with a deal." Owner/occupiers almost always fall in love with the deal, so they pay more. (By the way, the term owner/occupier is pronounced "owner occupier" not "owner slash occupier." It's appropriate for residential or commercial properties.)

What's the bottom line of all this? For any property you're interested in, you must look at your answers to the table on page 40, and see how that property fits in with your needs. Add items that are important to you. If it's not a good fit, move along. If you're not sure, ask people whose opinion you trust— a real estate professional, lawyer, banker, or other investors. Don't blindly take their advice, but ask them to share with you their reasoning process. You'll learn a lot, even if you don't take their recommendation.

5

The Inside Scoop on Real Estate Loans

Once you identify the type of property you want to buy, you should learn a little bit about the different kinds of lenders who hold mortgages on that type of property. This is because your tactics for finding out about the foreclosures, and your approach to negotiating with the lender, will vary depending on their category.

Individuals

Starting with the simplest lender, individual people loan money secured by real estate. Most often this happens when a property owner sells to a buyer and then *carries the financing,* or agrees to accept payments over time instead of demanding the purchase price, in full, at closing. Sometimes it's because the buyer is not credit-worthy enough to borrow money from a traditional source. Other times it's because the seller doesn't want cash because the money would just sit in a bank, earning low interest rates.

Occasionally, people will loan out money on mortgages to strangers, just like the banks do. Many people who have cash to invest simply loan it out to people for a higher interest rate than a savings account would earn. Sometimes these people make bad loans and have to foreclose.

Financial Institutions

Banks, credit unions, and mortgage companies also loan money on real estate. Years ago, people went down the street to their local savings and loan, and borrowed money from the same banker who handled their savings account. Then, for the next twenty years, they made their payments each month to that same bank. If they had a financial problem, they called their loan officer (who probably went to the same church), in order to work things out.

Today, everything is different. Whatever friendly face you do business with in order to borrow money is usually just an *originator*. They're called that because all they do is originate, or start the loan. Once all the documents are signed and the money changes hands, many originators sell the loan to large investors on what's called the *secondary market*. (Don't assume there's something called the *primary market*, because there isn't.)

Someone still has to collect the payments, make sure the borrower has insurance in place, and all the other little things having to do with the administration of a loan. This stuff is called the *servicing*. Whoever does the servicing gets paid a fee by whomever owns the loan.

> **Insight:**
> Any loan can be split up into pieces. Different companies have different decision-making authority regarding the same mortgage. Don't take it personally when you're shuffled from person to person as you try to obtain foreclosure information. It's like a scavenger hunt—a piece here, a piece there, until you have everything. Be persistent; you'll be rewarded in the end.

Selling a loan is called *selling the paper*. The buyer depends on whether the the paper is A-paper, B-paper or C-paper. *A-paper* means that it's a grade-A loan to a terrific borrower with a fantastic credit score. It usually has a low interest rate because there's little risk for the lender that the loan might go bad. *B-paper* consists of loans to less credit-worthy borrowers at higher interest rates. *C-paper* has the highest credit risk and the highest interest rates.

Why is this important to you? Lenders who specialize in B- or C-paper will have the riskiest loans, the most defaults, and the most foreclosures. If you want to cultivate relationships with lenders who might have lots of *troubled loans*, then you want to meet the B- and C-lenders. On the other hand, A-paper probably has the most equity and will give you the best opportunities to work something out.

Remember, though, whatever company is doing the foreclosure is probably not the lender who made the loan in the first place. You should know the originators in town, because they'll be your source of funds if you want to finance a purchase, but usually they will not be able to give you leads about foreclosures.

Governmental Sources

Your federal, state, and local governments loan money on real estate. Some of these programs are literal gold mines if you want to buy a property at foreclosure to use as a residence. Some federal programs, for example, will finance up to 95% of the foreclosure purchase price for you, and pay a 5% real estate commission. If you're a licensed real estate agent, you get the commission. That means you get into the property with nothing down. Chapter 18 gives more information on government foreclosures.

Institutional Lenders

Depending on how ambitious you are, you might run into some of the truly huge lenders. These are lenders like insurance companies and retirement funds. They've got massive amounts of money coming in the front door every day. It's hard work putting it out in good investments, so they place lots of money into loans. Sometimes those loans go bad, too.

The Paperwork

In addition to the wide variety of lenders, there are many different types of real estate loans, and an immense variety of paperwork. Every single real estate loan must have at least two documents—a *promissory note* and a *security instrument*. Security instrument is a generic term. The specific instrument could be a *mortgage* or a *deed of trust*, depending on the state where the land is located. The difference has to do with the technicalities of how a lender is able to use real estate as security for a loan. The differences are not important, except as they relate to the mechanics of a foreclosure auction. What's important right now is that the note and the mortgage or deed of trust are two separate documents with their own obligations.

By signing a promissory note, a borrower agrees to repay all the money borrowed, plus interest, late fees, and collection expenses if there's a default. When he or she signs a mortgage or deed of trust, it constitutes an *additional* and *separate* agreement that the lender can take the property if the loan isn't repaid. Many times people will say their mortgage payments are a certain amount but, technically, their *note* payments are that amount.

Once the lender exercises its rights under the mortgage, and takes property, then that instrument ceases to exist. On the other hand, the promissory note is alive and well, and the lender can still pursue collection activities.

Here's an example. A homeowner buys a house for $85,000. She puts $5,000 down and borrows $80,000. She signs a promissory note and a mortgage. The day after closing, she tears up the backyard and digs a giant hole in order to build a swimming pool. Unfortunately, she then runs out of money. She never makes the first payment on the note, and the bank forecloses. At that point, because of the mess it's in, the property appraises for only $60,000. The bank is the only bidder at the auction, and bids 80% of the appraised value, or $48,000.

The reason for the discount is because the bank's appraiser can't get inside the house to see what shape it's in. His $60,000 appraisal is based only on what he can see from the outside, and an assumption that the inside is still okay. He might be wrong, though. No bank wants to bid on a property at foreclosure for $60,000, give the borrower a $60,000 credit on their promissory note, and then find out the house has been trashed and is worth only $40,000. That's why they bid less than the full amount of the appraisal.

The bank gives the homeowner credit for a $48,000 payment, leaving a balance due under the note of $32,000. It's called a *deficiency*. In most states, the bank can now sue the former homeowner for $32,000, plus interest and costs of collection, such as attorney's fees.

> **Insight:**
> Most homeowners and small business people think a note and mortgage are the same thing, all rolled up into one concept. Because of that, they also believe a foreclosure, or the alternative of voluntarily giving their property to the bank, ends matters. Because they don't understand that the promissory note survives, and they face liability for a deficiency, they aren't as motivated as they should be to work with you. If you understand this, then you'll understand why it's necessary to educate borrowers about the potentially terrible consequences of not working with you.

Grading the Property Owner

The greater the potential deficiency, the more motivated the property owner should be to work with you. In analyzing any opportunity, you should assign a grade to the property owner's degree of motivation. If you have a terrific chance to buy some property, but the owner isn't very motivated, then you're going to have to work ten times as hard and might still end up with nothing. That's why I like to think about seller motivation early in the process. I use the following scores: A—highly motivated; B—somewhat motivated, but won't work really hard; and, C—doesn't care one way or another.

If Jim were to analyze his three opportunities in terms of owner motivation, it might look something like this.

- ◆ Post Office—Probably a "B" because this is a terrific investment with a potentially nationwide pool of buyers. With the US government as a tenant, investors don't need to look at the particular building, just a copy of the lease. In all likelihood, there won't be any deficiency at all, because there's no reason to bid a discounted amount.
- ◆ Chiropractor—I'd say this would be a "C" motivation without some additional work on your part. The owner is probably a small and unsophisticated investor. He is the one least likely to understand deficiencies, and most likely to think his misery ends with a foreclosure.
- ◆ Homeowner—Usually an "A" motivation because of the fear of losing their home and ruining their credit. Introducing them to a concept like deficiency could sent them right over the edge into outright panic and bankruptcy, so be careful how you bring up the subject.

In a very few states, lenders aren't allowed to collect a deficiency after foreclosing on the borrower's principal residence. On the other hand, the foreclosure itself can ruin someone's credit, so there's still lots of motivation to work with you.

6

When Good Loans Go Bad

Typically, a struggling borrower will have a history of late payments and missed deadlines on his or her mortgage loan. Eventually, the lender will decide that the borrower is in trouble and won't be able to recover. There's no rule for how past due someone has to be before the foreclosure process starts.

Instead, the tolerance for delinquent payments depends on who owns the loan and the size of the unpaid balance. If a small bank loans millions of dollars to someone, then a sizeable percentage of the bank's net worth is tied up in one loan. There's a lot riding on that loan not going bad. As a result, the borrower and the lender will work really hard with each other to work something out and avoid foreclosure. There's a common saying—*If you owe one hundred thousand dollars, the bank owns you. If you owe one hundred million dollars, you own the bank.* The numbers vary, but the concept is sound. Find a large troubled loan owned by a small bank, and you'll find people who want to work with you to find a solution.

Because of strict federal regulations, banks are required to value loans differently, depending on how past due they are. In addition, banks are required to maintain certain asset levels in order to avoid being closed by the regulators. Assets consist largely of loans. If a bank has $10 million in loans it's made to people, then it has $10 million in assets. A $1 million mortgage loan that goes into foreclosure might bring only $600,000 for the property. At that point, the bank has $600,000 in cash from the borrower (or a $600,000 piece of property) and a deficiency claim for another $400,000. The deficiency claim can't be counted as an asset. This is called *writing down the asset*. As a result, after foreclosure, the bank doesn't have $10 million in assets any more, it has $9.6 million.

It's important to understand this concept because it gives you a glimpse into the mind of a lender. You might be dealing in smaller numbers, but banks still hate to write down assets. Understanding the other side's pressures and motivations will always help you in negotiations.

Loans in Securitized Pools

For those loans which have been sold into large *securitized pools* at the national level, foreclosure is usually pretty much automatic once the borrower is a certain number of days past due. Most of the home mortgages fall into this category.

The reason foreclosure happens so quickly with such loans is because of what's referred to as the *fooling with it factor*. Companies called *servicing agents* manage the pool in return for a small fee on each loan. In order to manage a securitized pool efficiently, the agent can't waste time working with borrowers to help them out of their troubles, because the fee is too small. In other words, the servicing agent can't afford to *fool with* the troubled loan.

They also can't spend a lot of time and money chasing borrowers after a foreclosure in order to try to collect a deficiency (the remaining unpaid balance) on the promissory note. Finally, they also can't waste a lot of time and money trying to sell a piece of foreclosed real estate. As a result, these are terrific sources for foreclosure properties. Managers of securitized pools are highly motivated to let you solve their problems for them.

Work the Workout Department

Other lenders, who manage real estate loans at the local level, might be more flexible with a troubled loan. With large regional banks, the loan might be transferred to something called *special assets* or the *workout department*. In banking, a loan is called an asset because it's something valuable. Special assets have problems that require a lot more attention and closer supervision than is typical.

Insight:

Workout departments do not want to rehabilitate a person to financial well-being and then keep them as a customer. The borrowers are damaged goods. The bank wants them gone, or worked out of the bank. The good news for you about special assets and workout departments is that the bank employees working there generally have more discretion, creativity, and authority than other loan personnel.

If a branch manager tells you he or she can't accept less than the full amount to pay off a mortgage, it's because that's all the authority he or she's been granted. He or she has to do several hours worth of paperwork to get permission to do anything different. That's several hours not spent on getting new customers or doing the many other things that must be done. So, the easy answer to you is, "No, we can't accept less than the full payoff even though everybody knows the property's worth only half of that."

If you can get a loan transferred into the special assets or workout department, you'll meet with greater success. In the alternative, you could talk to the lower-level employee and find out what's required to obtain permission to accept less than full payment on a mortgage. Then, you could write up all the paperwork—usually an analysis of the property value and the borrower's other assets and income—needed by the powers that be.

The Bank's Prepwork

If the bank decides that a borrower is going to be foreclosed, there are several preliminary items of information and procedures the bank must follow before it can actually foreclose on the property. You, too, need to be aware of what is happening during this time, so you can make informed decisions as well.

First, the lender has to obtain a *title report* on the property. This shows the current owner of the property and all recorded liens. The original borrower might have sold the real estate to someone else without paying off the mortgage. If there are IRS liens, then the lender must give the IRS a certain number of days notice before it can foreclose, otherwise the tax lien will remain on the property. The borrower might have borrowed additional money against the property and allowed a second mortgage on it. All these things will show up on the title report.

The first lender to record a mortgage is in the *first position* or *has a first lien*. Everybody who records after that is a *junior lienholder*. If the first lienholder forecloses, then it *wipes out* all the junior lienholders (except the IRS—but more about that, later). The second mortgage, for example, just disappears. It doesn't exist any more. The borrower still owes the money, because he or she signed a *promissory note*, but that's separate from the mortgage.

On the other hand, if a junior lienholder forecloses, he or she just wipes out the lienholders that came *after* him or her. A foreclosure purchaser who buys from the junior lienholder buys a piece of real estate that is still subject to the senior liens. To keep the property, the purchaser has to pay the first mortgage *in addition to* whatever was paid to the junior lienholder.

Before a foreclosure, the lender will also obtain either an *appraisal* of the property or something called a *broker price opinion*. An appraisal is a somewhat scientific guess about how much a willing buyer would pay a willing seller for the property. It might involve analysis of the sale of similar properties in the recent past, how much and how reliable the income stream is, what it might cost to build a similar property, and many other factors. Chapter 12 tells you how to perform your own informal appraisal.

A *broker price opinion*—called a BPO for short—is a real estate broker's unscientific opinion about how much a property is worth. Whereas an appraiser might take two months and charge the lender $1,000 for an appraisal of a three-bedroom, two-bathroom house, the real estate broker might have a general idea that all such houses in similar neighborhoods sell for around $125,000, depending on the condition of the house. Which method the lender uses depends on how complicated the property is.

The lender needs this information so it will know how much to bid at the foreclosure auction. Just because the bank loaned $100,000 against the property last year doesn't mean it's worth $100,000, or anything approaching that, today. If the lender is the high bidder at the foreclosure auction, then it must give the borrower a credit against the loan, in the amount of the bid.

The Path to Foreclosure

There are generally two different paths to foreclosure, depending on the state where the land is located. In *nonjudicial* states, the mortgage contains something called a *power of sale*. Someone has been given the authority to sell the property at a foreclosure. Usually, states that use deeds of trust have nonjudicial foreclosures. *Judicial foreclosure* states require a lawsuit and a court order before the property can be sold. Those states usually employ mortgages rather than deeds of trust. Some renegade states use mortgages with powers of sale.

Be aware that the federal government has made several attempts to create separate, federal foreclosure laws. These would apply to all federal loans, whether the agency originated the loan or acquired it by other means. The goal is to standardize nonjudicial foreclosure, even in states that currently employ judicial foreclosure. In addition, federal loans would typically have shorter advertising times, greater leniency for mistakes, and greater latitude to collect deficiencies. The federal laws proposed, but not yet passed, are not consumer protection laws, they are federal lender protection laws. To track such laws, check with your congressman.

In *power-of-sale* states, upcoming foreclosures must be advertised in some sort of public way. They generally fall into three categories:

1. advertisements in the legal section of local newspapers or specialized newspapers devoted to legal notices;
2. preforeclosure documents recorded in the real estate records; or,
3. notices posted on a bulletin board at the courthouse.

You may see a foreclosure advertised several different times, for several different dates. For example, the first time you notice an advertisement about a property that interests you, it might say the foreclosure is set for April 23rd. Then, you'll see the same property advertised for May 29th. This could go on for a while.

The reason for this usually has to do with technicalities. The law doesn't favor taking people's property away from them, so it requires that everything be done *just exactly right*. A typo in the ad (even about something very minor) might make the whole notice defective. The lender will have to start all over.

Getting ready for a foreclosure is a time-consuming and paperwork-intensive process. There are many opportunities for mistakes. Mistakes generally lead to lawsuits. In theory, lenders are always well-motivated to work things out with someone in order to avoid the foreclosure sale. In practice, this depends on the size of the loan, the number of other problems that need attention, and the length of a lender's workday.

Contrary to popular belief, lenders don't want to grab real estate and sell it at a profit. In fact, when lenders sell foreclosed property at a profit, they almost always get sued because the borrower feels abused and cheated. Usually, the borrower wins those lawsuits, receiving large damage awards. If you understand that banks are *afraid* to make a profit on foreclosures, then you'll have one of the most valuable pieces of inside information in this whole industry.

7

Find Troubled Properties, Early

Unless some lender violates its customer's privacy, you generally won't be able to find troubled properties before they become public knowledge. The trick, then, is for those borrowers to find you. You want to generate prospects by making yourself easy to find.

There are three efficient and economical ways for people to find you:

1. word-of-mouth referrers (your fan club);
2. seminars and newsletters; and,
3. targeted advertising—small yard signs, etc.

Get to Those Who Need You

Word of mouth might not bring you the most inquiries, but it will bring you the most business. That's because word of mouth generally carries with it an implied recommendation, so the borrower is already predisposed to believe you can help him or her. Unfortunately, if you're just starting out in buying foreclosures, you don't yet enjoy any word-of-mouth reputation.

Seminars and newsletters let you promote yourself without sounding really obvious about it. The recipients of your efforts pay attention because they have a problem, or know someone who has a problem. As a result, they're predisposed to seek help, but you still have to convince them you're the person who can deliver.

> **Insight:**
> For some strange reason, people respect advice more if they have to pay for it. You don't have to charge much, but it should be *something*. Seminars and the newsletters can provide a tidy little supplement for your income and can even help bankroll your first foreclosure purchase.

If you're a people-person and can comfortably speak in front of groups, then a seminar is the best vehicle for you. If you enjoy meeting with people, but don't like public speaking, then you can create a *meet the expert* seminar-type function. Someone else introduces you and then people mill about, eat cookies, and drink punch while you wander around and just talk. If you're not comfortable with either one of these, then go with the newsletter or informative article route.

Some people will learn enough from you to avoid foreclosure. That's okay—it's a positive result for you. Every seminar attendee or newsletter subscriber who's able to learn from you and solve their own problems is a powerful and motivated referrer totally convinced of your credibility and value.

Sadly, most people, for emotional or other reasons, will not be able to implement the advice you give them. Those people will become your preforeclosure customers.

The most calls, the fewest prospects, and the biggest expense, will come from advertising. That's because most of your advertising-related calls will be from people who are merely curious, or who are only days away from losing their property. Also, you must work really hard to differentiate yourself from all the other preforeclosure advertisers, some of whom operate on a nationwide level.

Enlist the Lender

The first person to learn that a loan is headed towards foreclosure is the lender. You'd think the borrower would know first, when he or she fails to make the monthly payments, but borrowers are generally very optimistic people.

They expect a miracle to happen, and everything will then be rosy. The lender knows better. But bankers have very strict privacy laws, and can't go around discussing past-due accounts.

This is not to say that you shouldn't talk to lenders. It just means that you must rely on two separate sales jobs. You must sell the lender on the idea that you can help. Then, you must rely on the lender to sell the borrower on the idea that you can help. You want the lender to encourage the borrower to contact you. Why would they do this? Because banks do not want real estate. They call it the *owned real estate,* or sometimes *ORE,* or even sometimes *REO* (real estate-owned) portfolio. It is a lot of work for the bank to own, insure, maintain, and generally fool with real estate they never intended to own in the first place.

Armed with the lender's natural reluctance to foreclose, and then fortified with your personal professionalism, credibility, and sincerity, you are going to sell the lender on giving a single piece of paper to the borrower. That's all— just one sheet of paper.

An example of a flyer you want the lender to hand out for you is on page 67. Before preparing your own, however, you need to set up some relationships with lenders that will foster their giving your flyer to their troubled customers. You need to sell yourself to them. In the beginning, this is a numbers game, like most sales. You must get your *product* (meaning YOU) in front of as many people as possible. Some of them will buy. Most of them won't. The more people you contact, the more *sales* you'll have.

This is my personal, always successful, approach to sales:

- make contact;
- establish credibility;
- create a relationship;
- ask for permission to sell; then,
- sell.

Here's the blueprint for getting to talk to the lender.

Make Contact

The first thing you want to do is *build a database of lenders*. Call all the banks and credit unions in town and find out who's in charge of their real estate loans for your area of interest. (Commercial lenders are separate people from residential lenders.) Many times they specialize by size, usually called *small*, *mid-range*, and *large*. It will change from bank to bank, so you just have to ask lots of questions. The vice presidents who handle subdivision development loans are different from the ones who make loans to homeowners, even though both involve single-family homes. In larger banks, there's usually also a completely separate department for community *redevelopment loans*, also called *affordable housing loans*. Many, but not all banks have something called a *Special Assets Department*. Special Assets handles loans in default.

Put all of these names, titles, and lenders in some sort of database on your computer so you can easily merge them into a letter. Make a note of any names that might be male or female, like Terry Collins, Dale Robinson, or M. D. Smith. Ask the receptionist the gender of these people, so you can make a note. (Nothing will mark you faster as an amateur than addressing a letter to Mr. Terry Collins, who happens to be a woman.)

Establish Credibility

You might not use many of the concepts in your personal investing, but believe me, someone's going to ask you questions about them. You'd be stunned how many people, upon finding out I'm a commercial real estate broker, ask me about current FHA home loan interest rates. "How should I know," I want to say, "I don't sell houses." But, I don't say that. I just keep up with FHA interest rates, so I don't lose credibility when people ask me those questions.

Being familiar with matters that relate to your industry, if not directly to you, is a simple way to establish credibility with someone. The more credibility you have in general, the more you establish with a lender you want to help you. Some other ways this credibility is established includes the following.

Promote yourself as an expert

Go to your church, civic group, YMCA, or Chamber of Commerce and offer to give a speech or write an article about "Helping Loved Ones Who Might Be Facing Foreclosure." The title shouldn't be "Avoiding Foreclosure," because that's a little too blatant for most people. (Would *you* want a co-worker accidentally observing you reading an article entitled "How to Avoid Foreclosure?") Make the title of your talk positive and proactive. Remember, this is about helping people who may be in a crisis.

Build experience as a speaker or writer

You can do this pretty quickly—it doesn't take very many speeches or articles. I think three would do the trick. Book clubs or retirement community newsletters might be good places to start.

> **Insight:**
> Practice on groups of people who won't carry tales if you botch things or stammer the first time you try public speaking.

Create a professional appearance for your communications

Create some letterhead on your computer. If you don't have a business address where you can receive personal mail, then it's best to get a P.O. Box rather than use a home address. I think I'm like most people, and if I see a business with an address of "11861 Heatherwood Lane," then I assume that person is not quite legitimate. (I'm usually wrong, but it's a common prejudice.)

Use a dedicated business telephone or your cell phone number. You don't want children answering the phone when people call you. Be honest and ask your boss if you can use your direct telephone line at work for these types of calls. Even if it's not allowed, he or she will remember you had the integrity to ask, and might refer business to you. If you use your cell phone, avoid *cute* greetings for your voicemail.

Be sure to include an email address (that you check regularly), but not one like bighotmomma@email.com or monasmommie@fastmail.com.

Remember, credibility is key. Most Internet services allow you to create multiple user names.

You start to create a relationship with the lender from the first contact. How the relationship develops often depends on the credibility you have established for yourself as a workout specialist and on the repeated contacts you make with the lender. Begin by writing.

Create a Relationship

What follows is a sample of a form letter that you can create to send to lenders and other referrers. Tailor it to your particular situation and your writing style. The things in *italics* are notes to yourself—things to think about. (*Don't* include them in your letter.)

This letter <u>does not </u>sell your foreclosure services, so don't modify it and try to accomplish that goal. This letter is simply to make contact, establish credibility, and create name recognition. That's all.

Sample Letters to Create Name Recognition

Date

Internal Address

Dear Mr. or Ms. Whoever:

Alternative letter one:

Enclosed are two complimentary tickets to my upcoming seminar, "How to Help a Loved One Who Might be Facing Foreclosure." I would be honored if you would be my guest, and perhaps share with me—and the attendees, if you desire—your thoughts on a banker's perspective. If you are unable to attend, please feel free to give these tickets to someone else. My seminar is purely educational. No products or services will be offered for sale, nor will attendees be contacted afterwards in order to solicit business.

Alternative letter two:

Enclosed is a copy of my most recent article on "How to Help a Loved One Who Might be Facing Foreclosure." Please feel free to share it with members of your community or civic group who might be interested in the subject. This article does not promote the sale of any goods or services. It is purely educational and offered as a community service. As you can see from reading the article, it does not solicit any business, or promote any particular political, social, or religious agenda.

Closing paragraph for either letter:

Thank you for your time and interest. I look forward to an opportunity to meet with you sometime in the near future and hear your thoughts about successful debt workout strategies for troubled loans.

Sincerely,

John Smith

Mortgage Workout Specialist

Send a series of letters to potential referrers. You want to send about three of these letters, so the lender will start to recognize your name. Don't send the exact same letter each time. (It can start to look like junk mail.)

Ask for Permission to Sell

After the third letter, call the lender and *ask for an appointment*. Tell him or her that you will need about fifteen minutes of his or her time to talk about your mortgage workout services. This provides enough information to evaluate if he or she wants to meet with you or not, and whether he or she has the time.

Some people will advise you not to tell the lender the purpose of the meeting, because he or she will perceive you as a salesman and give you the brush-off. My opinion is you will just get the brush-off at the meeting if that is what is going to happen. Then it is even harder to overcome resistance, especially when the person feels surprised and ambushed.

In sales, it's *always* best to get permission to make the sales presentation. Otherwise, you're wasting time, and you can't afford that. Remember, too, you want a reputation as an ethical and straightforward person. You can't earn that by tricking people into meeting with you.

Prepare for your meeting

Before your first meeting, prepare an outline of what you will say. Practice a few times with friends, family, or the bathroom mirror, so you sound polished and smooth, but not memorized.

Insight:
Everyone can sell! You just have to believe in your product. When you brag about your children, you're selling. If you show off homegrown tomatoes, you're selling. Explaining to a police officer your really good excuse for speeding is selling. Once you truly understand the good deeds you can accomplish while also achieving your goal of earning money, **you'll be able to sell this program**.

Use buzzwords

Structure your presentation so you have the opportunity to use some buzzwords that showcase your knowledge and sophistication. Your presentation to the banker should start with your name and then your experience in giving seminars or writing articles. Tell the lender that you are a mortgage workout specialist. Share the observation that, nine times out of ten, people are too far gone in their troubles to engage in an effective workout to save their property, and they must therefore look at solutions that involve *sale of the asset*. That's a banker term. It means selling the real estate. It's imperative that you use banker language when talking to bankers. Otherwise, you have no credibility.

Practice on your least likely prospects

If you have several lenders you can meet with, start with the one who is *least likely* to send you business or *least likely* to loan you money to buy foreclosures. You want to practice on him or her. It's a freebie, because you're not blowing any opportunities if you mess up.

Leave something in the banker's hands

Give the banker your one-page flyer, similar to the one on page 67. Ask if he or she would mind sharing it with people who might be interested in one of your seminars or newsletters.

Don't overstay your welcome, and don't ask for business

Chat for a few minutes, thank him or her for his or her time, and leave. Don't overstay your welcome! The purpose of this meeting is to put a piece of paper in the lender's hand, so he or she will agree to put it in someone else's hands. You do not want the lender doing the selling for you and he or she is not allowed to tell you about defaulted loans.

Send a thank-you note

This is critically important—*before* the meeting, handwrite a thank-you note, address it, and stamp it. If you wait until after the meeting, you could be delayed or forget. Be prepared. Don't gush—you need about three sentences, tops.

> *It was a pleasure talking with you today. Thanks for giving me some of your time. I look forward to the possibility of being of service. Warmest regards, _____*

This *must* be handwritten. Print if your writing is terrible. As you leave the building from your meeting, drop the note in the nearest mailbox. People never send thank-you notes any more. It's a memorable occasion when someone receives one.

Sell

Having the lender hand out your flyer is the sale you are trying to make. Everything you have done up to your meeting and what you do after the meeting is all to get the sale. To make it work, you need a flyer. Craft something similar to what follows on the next page.

Jane Jones
Mortgage Workout Specialist
Offering confidential, low-cost consultation services
to people having problems with their real estate or home loans.
Free initial interview.

We are not bankruptcy lawyers or high-interest rate lenders.
We do offer advice about a wide variety of alternatives, *some* of which
include:
Loan Re-Structuring
Forbearance Agreements
Creditor Arrangements without Bankruptcy
Fast and Discreet Real Estate Sales
Debtor Protection

If we can't help you, we can refer you to other ethical professionals in the legal, accounting, and banking fields.

Please call or email for a free initial meeting or for a
complimentary copy of our newsletter,
"How to Help a Loved One Who Might be Facing Foreclosure"
[address, phone number, email address]

Follow up

The process is ongoing. If you don't already do so, start reading the business page of your newspaper. I can't tell you, specifically, what to look for, but you'll start seeing things that are relevant to you. It might be something like an article about money problems a company's having. Perhaps you'll see something about changes in foreclosure laws. It could be any number of things. Get in the habit of reading this section.

In addition, the business pages usually contain a section with press releases for promotions, awards, and other things about local professionals. Cut out any article about bankers on your list. Add the information to your database about that person.

If you happen to have an article about a lender before you have actually contacted him or her, include it in your initial letter like the one on p.63. Include an additional paragraph in your letter saying something like:

> *By the way, I thought you'd like an extra copy of the newspaper piece about* _____. *Congratulations!*

If you see the lender's name in the newspaper again or after you have had a meeting (unless he or she has been arrested, getting divorced, or something else unpleasant), cut out the article and mail it to him or her, along with your business card that contains the title "Mortgage Workout Specialist."

Send new copies of the flyer, in case the copy you have already left has been given to someone else. The goal is to gently, and regularly, remind him or her that you exist, but without any overt sales pitches. When an opportunity comes up, the lender will remember you and give someone your flyer.

Other Groups of Referrers

Bankers are just one group of referrers on whom you can concentrate. Others might include the following.

- *Divorce lawyers.* They generally encounter high concentrations of people with money problems. They also usually don't practice bankruptcy law or debt workout, so they'll be glad to refer people to you for help.
- *Ministers.* Like bankers and lawyers, they can't give you any names, but they do come to know about people in trouble. A minister is generally a nurturing person who wants to help, so

he or she will be motivated to give your flyer to other people, should they need your services.

◆ *Self-storage operators.* When people see a possible foreclosure looming, many of them start putting stuff in storage, just in case. They're also remarkably candid with the manager about financial problems motivating them to seek storage.

◆ *Title, pawn, pay check advance, and quick-cash businesses.* These businesses get to hear a lot of sad stories. Sometimes they simply can't loan additional money to someone in trouble, but they can hand out a flyer.

Insight:

There are plenty of categories of people who could be referrers. Use your imagination, but concentrate on particular types. That way, you can learn the language of their industry, establish comradery and empathy, and perhaps send business to *them*.

Seminars

I'm going to share with you some strategies for educating the public about your services through seminars, small meetings, newsletters, and informative articles.

If you decide to conduct seminars, you should limit them to two hours. One hour will be for your presentation and one hour will be for questions and answers. Usually you can rent a meeting room at a church or Chamber of Commerce pretty cheaply. Sometimes community colleges donate meeting rooms if you give out some free student tickets.

Be sure to contact your local newspaper's Community Events editor with the information about your seminar, and the information that a *limited number of free tickets* are available by calling a certain phone number.

Ask another professional to come with you to the meeting. Some people might have bankruptcy questions, so it's a good idea to have a bankruptcy lawyer present. Others might be interested in lenders who specialize in people with bad credit—usually a consumer protection group can provide you with an expert in that subject.

Whoever you invite to the seminar as a cospeaker should be someone who you've already prequalified as someone with the same high ethical standards that you have.

Before the seminar, estimate how many people you think will attend. Pull out that many business cards, plus a few extra. *Handwrite* on the back of each one the title and date of your seminar. As people enter the meeting room, shake their hands, introduce yourself, and hand them your business card.

If you leave materials sitting out on a table for people to pick up afterwards, most of them won't do it. That's because they don't want anyone thinking they are too interested in the subject. On the other hand, a business card can be slipped discreetly into a pocket or purse and consulted later. Because you've written the title and date of your talk on the back, they'll also remember who you are when they pull a strange card out of their purse two weeks later.

I recommend you charge some small fee for the seminar. Unfortunately, people feel that advice is more valuable if they have to pay something for it. They'll gladly pay a lawyer $150 an hour for the same consultation you're willing to give out for free. Start out charging about $10 per person. Give out lots of free tickets, if you have to, but tell people there's normally a fee.

If you're uncomfortable with public speaking, then introduce your guests and let them speak. Make sure you let everyone know *you're* in charge, though, and the go-to person if they're in trouble.

Remember, you're establishing credibility among a wide variety of people, most of whom will turn into referrers for you, and some of whom will turn into preforeclosure customers. All of these efforts are to get people to call you and psychologically give you permission to sell to them. You want to provide a community service and be helpful, but don't lose sight of your primary goal.

Lead Services and Advertising

Other methods for people to find you include lead services and advertising. Both can be expensive.

Lead Services

A lead service will sell you lists with names of people who have, in some manner, given permission to be contacted. They might have visited a website with information about avoiding foreclosure. Or, they could have called a toll-free number seen in national or local advertising. Somehow, they have expressed some sort of interest in foreclosures, they've given someone their contact information, and they've agreed that someone can get in touch with them.

You'll pay a certain amount per name in order to get this information. Usually, you have to buy packages of 100, 1,000, or 5,000 names. Then you call, write, or email these people and hope that they will contact you. Of course, everyone else who buys the lists will also be contacting them. I strongly discourage you from buying lists from these services. I, personally, think it's a waste of time and money, but you might have a different opinion.

Advertising

Traditional advertising is very good for some things. We all know Ford's "tough," but Mazda "zooms." These ads educate us about products and cause us to think of a specific product the first time a need arises. They're also incredibly expensive campaigns that rely on constant repetition. You can't afford that.

On the other hand, you can employ nontraditional, targeted advertising designed not to sell a product, but to generate a phone call or email in order to get someone in a database. In other words, you don't want your advertising to sell, you want your ads to simply help you identify people who *might* need your services. Selling comes afterwards.

This is the same reason I recommend putting on seminars. Your goal is to establish yourself as an expert and then get people to call you for help.

Your advertising can be done by placing ads in local thrift papers or in regular classified ads. I'd start out with the thrift papers (usually cheap or free) and then evaluate the response. If a thrift paper has a circulation of 1,000 people and you get ten good referrals, you might want to spend a little more money on an ad in a regular newspaper. If you get no leads at all from the thrift paper, then, odds are, it won't get any better by spending more money on a larger newspaper.

The ads that I've noticed are usually little blurbs like:

> *Facing foreclosure? We can help!*
> *Call 555-1234 to make an appointment for free consultation.*

Ads like this will get you calls from the desperate—the ones who are only days away from losing their property and are hoping for a miracle. You're not that miracle. You cannot evaluate a property, work out a solution, and implement it in days. If you know you can't finish, don't even start.

Better advertising can be accomplished by offering free advice within your ad. That's right—give something away for free and people will stop and take note. Many of them won't *think* they need you right now, but will call anyway, *just in case*. Some will suspect that a financial train wreck is looming in their lives, but can be avoided with proper planning. These people are your absolutely best prospects, because they've contacted you early enough for you to do some good.

Following are some ideas for ads. Be creative, but be serious! People with financial difficulties do not want to talk to anyone who thinks their situation is amusing. Cute ads will antagonize people. Be sure you put your own contact information at the bottom of each ad.

Sample Ads Promoting Your Services

Ask the Expert: My bank sent me a certified letter.
Are they getting ready to foreclose?

Many times, a certified letter is a technique to get your attention, so you take your loan seriously, call the banker, and try to get current. It's not always a signal that the end of the world is close at hand. Call or write for our free list of steps you should take when you get a certified letter from your lender.

Address/Phone Number/Email Address

Ask the Expert: Can I avoid foreclosure by giving the bank my property?

Almost always, the answer is NO! This is called a deed in lieu (pronounced "loo") of foreclosure. Legally, it's very risky for banks because of technical things having nothing to do with the value of your property. There are certain circumstances, however, where it can be the right solution. Call or write for our free list of steps you should take if you want to pursue this route.

Address/Phone Number/Email Address

Ask the Expert: How does foreclosure affect my credit?

Foreclosures stay on your credit report for seven years. They will typically lower your score by 100 points. This can be minimized with proper planning. Call or write for our free brochure explaining your credit reporting rights.

Address/Phone Number/Email Address

Ask the Expert: Which is worse on a credit report—bankruptcy or foreclosure?

Bankruptcy is always worse than foreclosure because it stays on your credit report much longer. Also, you can have one foreclosure, but maintain all your other credit. That looks good on a credit report as indicating that you had an isolated problem with a particular loan. Bankruptcy tends to seem like a global credit problem. Call or write for our free checklist for evaluating your options—bankruptcy or foreclosure.

Address/Phone Number/Email Address

The purpose of the ad is to establish credibility and to generate a contact. The trick will be to slim down all those contacts into the ones who are right for you—the ones who can be helped, but who won't be able to keep ownership of their property in the process. Notice I said "ownership." Many borrowers will be satisfied if they can continue to live in their own homes, or occupy their own business properties for some period of time until they can regroup, get over the trauma of impending foreclosure, and make plans for the future.

Other Ways to Find Distressed Properties

In all states, there must be some sort of public notice of foreclosure before a lender can proceed. Usually this is something in the "Legals" section of a newspaper classified section. Other times, it can be posted in the court house of the county or parish where the property is located. Besides the actual foreclosure notice, there are other early warning signs of a property owner in trouble. In states that use the deed of trust system, a lender might have to appoint a Successor Trustee before it can proceed. There are many other reasons for appointing a Successor Trustee, but it can be a clue of impending trouble. The tax collector's office can give you lists of delinquent real estate taxes—many times these same people are also delinquent on their mortgages. Divorces, IRS liens, judgment liens, and bankruptcy filings are also fertile fields for potential troubled properties. People at your local state and federal courthouses can tell you how to research these records to find what you need. (Chapter 8 covers researching preforeclosure notices in greater detail.)

Contacting Distressed Owners

If you find some distressed properties that you are interested in, you need to contact the owners. Send a letter to the property owner. You want the envelope to get his or her attention and beg to be opened. You also want it *not* opened by a secretary, in case the address is a business. Use a letter size envelope—the kind you would use for mailing a check to the water company, for example; handaddress it—don't use a computer; put your name in the return address (but not the name of your company); and, put the word "Personal" on the face of the envelope in large letters and highlighted in yellow. Don't put "Personal and Confidential" because all the bill collectors put that on their envelopes. Remember—discreet, but provocative. You want your letter opened by the addressee.

I have included a suggested letter on the following page. You can make up your own. The goal is to generate a phone call asking for more information. You never want to put too much information in the first letter. <u>This is not a sales letter</u>. It is a slim-down-the-suspects-into-prospects letter.

Insight:
False familiarity is a turn-off for most business people. Don't open a letter with "Dear Denise," for example, unless you know me well enough to invite me to join you for lunch some day. Begin business letters to strangers with "Dear Ms. Evans" and go from there.

Save a copy of all the letters you send out. File them alphabetically. You might not get a response from your letter, but end up hearing from these people through some other route. It's important to know if you ever sent them a form letter, in case the subject comes up.

Sample Contact Letter

Date

Internal Address

Dear Mr. or Ms. Whatever (If unsure of gender, the use of "Mr./Ms." is okay)

My name is _____. Please do not be embarrassed, but I offer ethical and compassionate solutions to problems with real estate loans. My initial consultation is free. I can often refer you to other pre-screened, ethical professionals in the fields of refinance, bankruptcy, or credit management. Other times, I might be able to arrange for a quick and discreet sale and leaseback of your property, allowing you to preserve your credit, your reputation, and your day-to-day affairs. In some instances, people simply want to sell their property and make a clean break—moving some place else in order to begin building better times and better memories.

Whatever your goals, you can rest assured that I am not just another opportunist trying to make money at your expense. If I can help, and we can both come out ahead, then we need to work together. If I can't help, then I can save you lots of time and anguish by referring you to people who can assist you. Please take that first step of putting yourself back in charge of your life—contact me for some additional information and possibly a personal consultation.

Sincerely,

[*your name*]
Mortgage Workout Specialist

8

Find Borrowers from Public Notices

Sometimes you don't have the resources or energy to engage in preforeclosure prospecting. Even if you do, many troubled borrowers will not know about your services. That's why you should stay informed regarding scheduled foreclosures. You're late into the game at that point, with lots of competition, but you can still buy good properties at fair prices.

The foreclosure early warning signs will vary depending on your jurisdiction. If you don't know which one you fall under, then call a *title company* and ask them. Title companies are involved in just about every real estate closing that gets done these days. As a consequence, they know a lot about the system and how things work.

Ask for Help

This is the first place in this book that relies heavily on you asking other people for advice. With so many different laws, it's just too hard to cover all the bases regarding the various ways of doing things. You'll need help.

When I have to ask someone for assistance, I always take doughnuts, Girl Scout cookies, or some other treat. It means, of course, you have to go in person to get your advice.

Once I'm able to see someone, I admit right away that I'm ignorant about a subject. I say I'm not looking for legal advice, just a general idea of *how things work.* If you try to impress people with how much you do know, you'll probably antagonize them.

After leaving, I drop into the nearest mailbox a thank-you note that's already been written and is just waiting for insertion of the right person's name. This absolutely, positively, depends on having the same pen for inserting the name as you used to write the letter. Nothing says "amateur" more than an obvious form letter with filled-in blanks.

Insight:

If I have to go back to the same source several times for help, I give Godiva Chocolates as a thank-you gift. Women love them. Men can always keep them for emergencies, like forgotten anniversaries. Nothing says "thank you" as memorably as one of those little gold boxes.

Torrens

Some states use a Torrens registration system for real estate in general, not just foreclosures. Under such a system, real estate titles are handled in a manner similar to car titles—there's one piece of paper with all the relevant information on it. This is the opposite of an *abstract system,* under which you have to examine many pieces of paper to find out who has claims against property.

A particular state isn't *either* Torrens *or* abstract. All states have some sort of abstract system. Some counties *also* use Torrens as a voluntary alternative to abstract.

For a Torrens registration, the process starts out in the courts. The property owner files a legal proceeding in which the nature of his or her title is stated along with all other claims or liens against the property. Claimants are given a certain number of days to contest that, or to claim that they, also, have an interest in the real estate. At the end of the process, there's a certificate of title issued, kind of like car titles. Any instrument affecting title to the land has to be noted on the certificate. No transfer is effective until it's recorded there. Usually, pre-foreclosure notices also have to be indicated on the certificate.

For counties that employ the Torrens system, call your local registrar's office and ask them how you can find out about preforeclosure notices. Sometimes, you have to physically go to where they are kept and read over the recent filings. That's not practical. More and more, I'm seeing this information available and searchable for free, online.

To find preforeclosure notices in abstract records, you usually have to search in a different office or website. Again, ask a title company or the mortgage loan department of a bank.

Remember that Torrens and abstracts are systems of recording things, not a system of foreclosure methods. In other words, your state may or may not require *anything* to be recorded before the foreclosure. All require public notices of some sort, but that might be a real estate record, a newspaper notice, or both.

Lis Pendens

Various states also conduct foreclosures differently. Some states require judicial foreclosures. It means that a court must issue an order so the lender can take the property. In those states, the lender will file a *lis pendens* notice either in the real estate records or with the Torrens registrar, as soon as it files the lawsuit. A really cautious lender will file both places, if possible.

NOTE: *There's federal legislation in the works to make all federal foreclosures (FHA, VA, etc.) nonjudicial, even in states that otherwise require judicial foreclosures. Be sure to keep track of developments in this area.*

Lis pendens is a Latin phrase that means "lawsuit pending." According to the system employed in our country, the public is put on constructive notice of all things recorded in the real estate records. If Joe sells land to Sue, Sue records her deed, and then ten minutes later Joe sells the same land to you, then you are *put on notice* that Joe didn't really own the land any more. Of course you can sue Joe, if you can find him, but you can't contest Sue's rights. She owns it. On the other hand, you're not required to know about all the lawsuits people file against each other, even if some of them are really important to the ownership of real estate.

As a result, the *lis pendens* system developed. If a lawsuit will affect the ownership of real estate, then you can file your notice and refer curious people to the actual lawsuit. Usually, it's a one-page affair that simply discloses a court and case number in order to get the details of the lawsuit. People file these notices for many reasons besides foreclosures. Boundary line disputes, divorces, squabbles among heirs, all sorts of things generate *lis pendens* notices.

To find them, search the real estate records and the Torrens records, if available. Again, call your local offices and ask them if they have searchable online databases. If not, ask them if they have searchable databases from terminals located at their offices or if they publish lists periodically of things that have been recorded. As an alternative, you can also employ one of the list services from the Internet. Their fees generally range from $20 a month to $100 a month, depending on how much information you want.

Court Actions

Another alternative in judicial foreclosure states is to search the lawsuit records themselves. This is easier than it sounds, because of the court forms a lawyer has to complete when he or she files a lawsuit. Just about every jurisdiction I know of requires plaintiffs to prepare something called, generically, a *Civil Action Cover Sheet*. It's a form that gives the court some basic information about the case.

Usually, the plaintiff, or claimant, will have to check a box on a preprinted form to indicate the type of litigation. That way, the court can keep statistics about quantities of lawsuits in its jurisdiction. It can also employ some sort of assignment system so that no single judge gets overloaded and so that judges with certain specialties can hear most of the cases in those areas.

Call your local courthouse and ask for the clerk's office where parties file judicial foreclosure suits. Some states call it "Circuit Court," some call it "District Court." There might be other names. Ask the clerk if there's a way to find foreclosure actions without having to read every paper filed that week. Sometimes, if the real estate recorder does not have a searchable database, the court system does. That Civil Action Cover Sheet information is usually keyed into the court database.

Once you find the judicial foreclosure notices, you can contact the property owner. Many times they're at home, simply waiting for the ax to fall. In order to buy time to evaluate their situation and negotiate with the lender, refer likely candidates to an attorney or a credit counseling agency. They can assist with preparing an *Answer* or perhaps a *Motion to Dismiss*. These are perfectly legal and ethical delaying tactics. Generally, they'll buy you another thirty days. You should check the law in your particular jurisdiction to make sure.

Nonjudicial Foreclosure States

Other states employ nonjudicial foreclosure. As long as the lender meets the strict requirements for *acceleration* (calling the note and demanding payment in full) and notice, it can auction the property without filing a lawsuit first. Some nonjudicial states also require a *lis pendens* notice. Some don't.

If there are no *lis pendens* filings, then your earliest public warning of an upcoming foreclosure will be the newspaper or courthouse notices. In most states, upcoming foreclosures must be advertised a certain number of times in a newspaper of general circulation. Sometimes the advertisement can be on a bulletin board at the courthouse.

A newspaper of general circulation might mean the one you read every morning or it might be one whose only purpose is to publish legal notices. It's usually cheaper to buy space in these specialized papers because their publishers don't have to support a lot of reporters, researchers, administrative people, and a huge building. When in doubt, call a title company and ask them where foreclosure notices are advertised.

As stated previously, you may see a foreclosure advertised several different times, for several different dates. For example, the first time you notice an advertisement about a property that interests you, it might say that the foreclosure is set for April 23rd. Then, you'll see the same property advertised for May 29th. Again, usually, the reason has to do with some sort of technicalities. An error in the ad, about something very minor, might make the whole notice defective. I've also seen foreclosures postponed for no other reason than a computer was down and no one could calculate the payoff. No matter what the reason, the whole process has to start over for the entire required number of notices.

The Notice

The foreclosure notice must contain at least six things in most states:

- the name of the borrower;
- the name of the lender;
- the book and page number where the mortgage is recorded;
- a legal description of the property;
- the date, time, and place of the foreclosure auction; and,
- the person who will conduct the auction.

Sometimes the street address will also be listed, but that is often kind of hit-or-miss. Some notices contain them, some don't. If I really wanted to, I could take the ad to the tax assessor's office and ask them to tell me the street address, or I could figure it out myself. That's a lot of work, though, and you have to ask some people to help you. Usually you can just call the person conducting the auction and ask them for the street address.

Why don't they publish the address in the notice? Foreclosures are really technical. If absolutely everything isn't done exactly correct, then they're no good. All a lender is *required* to do in most places is show the legal description. Legal descriptions never change. Street addresses change all the time. Where I live, for example, the city renamed River Road to Jack Warner Parkway. If a bank ran a foreclosure notice today and included a street address of 59867 River Road, then it would be incorrect.

Borrower

The borrower is the person who signed the note and mortgage. Someone completely different might own the property today, if the original owner sold *subject to* the mortgage.

Lender

The name of the lender doing the foreclosure isn't always the same as the original lender. Even if you're not interested in a particular property, make a note of the foreclosing lender. They may have other properties in the ORE (owned real estate) portfolio. You can call or write and ask for information.

Mortgage Instrument

I always like to look at the mortgage instrument itself, so the book and page number where it's recorded are important. Usually, the original loan amount is a good indication of the value of the property as of the date it was made. It's not true 100% of the time, because you can borrow more than the value of your house or land if you have steady income and a good credit score.

As a rule of thumb, the older the mortgage—the more equity the property owner has. Some people think that means you can get a better bargain when you buy the property at auction for the remaining balance of the loan. Beware! The instances of investors buying million dollar properties for $100,000 and are few and far between, and largely the stuff of urban legends. Almost all pre-foreclosure owners with large equities are going to file for bankruptcy before they allow their property to be taken by the bank for next to nothing. Even if they eventually lose their property through a bankruptcy sale, they buy time to market it properly and engage in an orderly sale process instead of a fire sale. In other words, they leave the bankruptcy sale with money in their pocket.

Legal Description

The legal description will give you some idea of the amount of land included. Most of the time, it will be a subdivision lot number only, but sometimes there'll be a *metes and bounds* description. That's the kind surveyors use. It usually goes something like this:

> Start at the northwest corner of the southeast quarter of the southwest quarter of Section 19...

Sometimes, at the end, it will tell you how many acres, more or less. If it doesn't, then you can usually make a drawing of the property lines and their distances and figure out the acreage. If the description makes a rectangle that's 330 feet on two sides and 450 feet on the other two sides, then you multiply 330 times 450 to get 148,500 square feet. An acre has 43,560 square feet. If you divide 148,500 by 43,560 you get a little over 3.4 acres.

Date, Time, and Place

The date, time, and place of the auction will generally be something like:

> January 15, 2006, between the hours of 9:00 a.m. and noon, on the steps of the Jefferson County Court House.

The reason they're not more specific is the lawyer might have ten foreclosures scheduled for the same day. He or she doesn't know in advance which ones will get postponed and which ones will have lots of bidders and a lengthy auction process. So, he or she keeps the timing flexible. Sometimes, you can call the office of the person conducting the auction the afternoon before a foreclosure and get a more definite time. If not, then you just have to be camped out at nine in the morning, waiting for him or her to show up. (By the way, if the court house has a lot of steps, find out where the lawyer's favorite *spot* is, so you can wait nearby.)

Auctioneer

Finally, the person who will conduct the auction is usually an attorney. He or she will not tell you anything about the property, the note, the value, or the payoff. The reason for this is that if any of the information is not fully correct, it opens up the possibility of litigation. It's not at all unusual for a lender (or its agent like an attorney) to make one tiny misstep and end up in years of litigation with a property owner. That's why they're so cautious.

The lawyer will tell you the terms of the auction sale. This is critical. Some lenders require you to pay your entire bid—in cash—on the date of the auction. Some require a large, cash down payment with the balance due in thirty days. If you don't pay the balance, you lose your deposit and the lender runs another foreclosure notice for a second auction.

I like to find out the name of the loan officer. The lawyer won't tell you, but sometimes his or her secretary will. Other times you just have to do some detective work. The reason I want to talk to the loan officer is I want to ask if he or she will consider financing some or all of the auction purchase price. Be bold. If the answer is "No," then ask why. Sometimes you get a young, inexperienced person, and he or she will actually tell you about problems with the property. Other times you'll get an education, and learn that the foreclosing entity doesn't make loans, it just buys them on the secondary market. It never hurts to ask.

Insight:

A non-threatening way to ask "Why?" is to say, "I'm always learning new things in this profession. Do you mind sharing with me your reasons for [what you want to know]?"

Use Your Systems and Procedures

Tape the foreclosure notice to a letter size piece of paper, because tiny slips of paper tend to get lost easily. Make a note with the name of any person you talked to, the date of the conversation, and the information they gave you. File these things in your tracking system. Enter the date of the auction on whatever calendar system you use.

9

Eliminate Potential Problems, Quickly

To be successful in handling foreclosed properties, you need tools to make decisions easier. You need to find ways to quickly eliminate potential properties from your list. There are usually too many properties to consider and not enough time to adequately research each, so you need some decision-making short cuts.

Make the Easy Cuts

Your first step will depend on what's the least trouble. Where I live, it's extremely easy to research property records and mortgages online. I do *that* first, because it gives me an idea about part of town, and about the approximate amount of the mortgage balance. If the mortgage is one year old, in the amount of $1,000,000, then odds are I can't afford it.

For those of you who have to hike down to the courthouse and look up information that I can get online, you might want to take a different first step. If you have, or can get, the street address, drive by the property. Notice the building—are there any *sudden death* items visible? What's the neighborhood like? Is there evidence of children, retirees, or students? Does it seem well-kept or run-down? What businesses are nearby? For example, if you're looking at a business property and you can see a branch bank or a McDonald's from the front door, it's almost always a great location. If you're looking for a home for yourself, and have children, then how far away are the schools? Is the house on a busy street or a quiet one? Do there seem to be other children in the area?

> ### Insight:
> In my experience, if anything about an opportunity makes you uncomfortable, reject the property. Call it intuition, a gut feeling, whatever you like. Both involve shortcuts in the brain. You see or hear something, your brain processes it in the background and compares it to other information or experiences, and out pops an instant opinion. Every time I've talked myself out of a gut feeling, something went wrong.

Is There Enough Time

Another instant reject area has to do with how much time remains before the auction. We call that the "window of opportunity." If the foreclosure is set for less than one week away, you can't do everything you need in such a short time. There's no point in wasting your time getting started.

Who's on the Other Side

As you gain more experience, you'll find other things that cause you to eliminate certain opportunities. I have some lenders I don't like. They might have great properties, in terrific parts of town, with lots of equity, but I just don't like their people. They're difficult, unreasonable, petty, and in love with stupid and useless paperwork. Life is just too short to spend any time on those lenders, so I don't.

Multiple Liens

For inexperienced buyers, I recommend not pursuing *preforeclosure properties* with more than one lien. If you live in an online county, you can go to the real estate records, type in the owner's name, and the computer should list all real estate transactions affecting that person. They might involve other properties, so you have to pick your way through and read property descriptions on instruments in order to match everything up. If your real estate records are not online, you can go to the recording office and look up the information. Sometimes title companies or real estate lawyers will give you title opinions relatively cheaply.

In my opinion, if a piece of real estate has more than one lien, then it's going to be complicated working with everyone. For a first or second deal, you're better off looking for something else.

Personal Pet Peeves

It's personal, I know, but I've got some other pet peeves. I don't like buying rental properties that are on septic tanks. As a result, I have maps that show where all the sewer lines go in my town. I know it sounds weird, having a sewer map, but how else am I going to instantly disqualify septic tank properties? The reason I'm prejudiced against them is because a septic tank requires a little care and maintenance, and a lot of common sense. Unfortunately, these things aren't important to the average renter, who will pour bacon grease down the kitchen sink even though it's deadly to a septic tank. Rather than be optimistic about human nature, I simply avoid the issue and look for houses on the sewer lines.

Gas lines and fireplaces are other red flags for me. I tend to think they'll lead to a renter burning my house down. It's irrational, I know, but they're my fears. You probably have some of your own. (I don't encourage taking investment risks as a therapy for overcoming phobias.)

Going to Round Two

If the property's survived the first cut, then it's time to contact the owner. Revisit the list you made earlier about what kind of property you want and all the sudden death items. Read the list; see if anything has changed in your opinion; and, make the appropriate corrections. You'll ask the sudden death questions in your very first telephone conversation with the owner.

10

Interview the Borrower

I want you to do an exercise. (You should practice this *every time* a new person contacts you and asks for your help. These are real people, with real problems, and they're facing one of the worst things that can happen to them.) Take five minutes. Think of the first person on your list of prospects. Visualize him or her on the day the particular property was purchased and then now see them scared and facing foreclosure. Look at them closely, back on that exciting day, and you'll see written in their face all the pride and optimism of property ownership.

I'm not kidding—I want you to do this every single time. These are real people with real feelings. No matter what you think about how much their situation might be their own fault, you cannot let that enter into your attitude. We've all made mistakes in judgment, we all have blind spots where we're incompetent at certain things, and we've all, at one time or another, unfairly suffered the consequences of something that was simply not our fault.

Saying that, you're not the personal life preserver for everyone who contacts you. If you can help someone and make money in the process, then help them. If you can't, then give them the name of some other professional who is appropriate for their particular situation.

The Initial Contact

When you answer your phone, you should answer with something like, "Good morning. This is Denise Evans." The "good morning" or "good afternoon" part is longer than a simple "hello" and gives the caller time to get used to your voice. Next, using your full name lets them know that they've reached the right person. People generally don't want to pour out their hearts until they know they've reached the right person.

The first thing you should do in the conversation is *find out how they heard about you*. How are you ever going to figure out the best method of marketing if you don't track where your prospects come from? In addition, fail to send a thank-you note to a referrer, just once, and see how quickly that source dries up.

There's no need to be sly about finding out the source of your referrals. I usually say something like, "Do you mind letting me know how you learned about me?" This usually allows the borrower to ease into the conversation about his or her problem, instead of starting out cold.

After the introductory things, it's time to get down to business. This doesn't mean selling your services over the phone. The phone should be used for only one thing—making an appointment. Resist the urge to rattle on about all the good you can do. You run the risk of the caller being so filled with anxiety that they hear about one-fourth of what you say. Then they get it all mixed up and tell their brother-in-law, and he renders an opinion that you're a quack and a thief! It's not fair, but you brought it on yourself by trying to sell over the phone.

Before the First Meeting

You don't want to do a lot of work before the first meeting. That's because a significant number of people will be unwilling or unable to use your services. If you invest a lot of time doing research before every meeting, then you'll wear out and get discouraged before you run across your first good deal.

The only thing you should do before the first meeting is to find out the answers to questions on your Instant Reject checklist from Chapter 3. Then, if you haven't already done so, ride around the property's neighborhood. If it's residential, then get a feel for the houses, cars, lawns, and activities. By activities, I mean, do there seem to be lots of children or students or retirees? Do the neighbors seem to be in each other's yards, visiting a lot? Does the seemingly quiet street become a thoroughfare during morning and evening traffic times? Make a few notes—after awhile, different properties will tend to run together in your mind.

If you're looking for something to buy for your own residence, and you have children, then you should also check out the school districts. Then ask yourself, "Does this look like a neighborhood where I'd like to live?"

For investment property, you want to note the surrounding businesses, houses, or apartments, and if the area is thriving or in decline. That's all, for the first drive-around.

If your first gut feeling does not have you feeling good about the property, call the owner *immediately*. Tell him or her that your specialty involves buying properties and structuring deals so the owner can walk away with relatively clear credit, no foreclosure, and perhaps some equity. You're able to do that because you have a very specialized list of property requirements. You've done some research, and his or her property doesn't fit into your profile. It has nothing to do with the loan, the value of the property, or whether it's a good purchase. It just doesn't fit into your model. Don't explain more than that. People tend to run on at the mouth too much, and it usually gets them in trouble.

It might seem more kind to attend the first meeting, be polite, think about it, and then refer the homeowner elsewhere, but it's not. That person is in a desperate and scary situation. He or she needs solutions more than good manners. You're holding out false hope, and wasting his or her valuable time, if you string this out.

What you *should* do is refer him or her to other people in your area who have different property profiles in which they're interested. Search the Internet to find networking groups of mortgage workout specialists in your community.

Insight:
If you conduct business in a moral and upright way, then you have nothing to fear from working *with* your competitors on some things, and *competing fairly* on other things.

The First Meeting

Schedule a one-hour meeting with a borrower at the property they are in danger of losing. Usually, it will be their home. This will be your first and best opportunity to get a good look at it. If they want to meet someplace else, find out why. It could be nothing more than the fact that they haven't told the children yet, and there's no privacy at the house. It could be that the place is radioactive and glows at night. You'll still need to see the property before too long, but don't press things if the owner doesn't want to meet there at first. You want the owner to be as comfortable as possible and willing to share information and be open to your suggestions.

During the first meeting, devote some amount of time to chatting. That's right, just sit and visit. You're looking for common ground, things that will allow you to relate to each other, person to person, as equals. Some people are awkward at small talk, so here are some pointers. These are not scripts or mechanical conversational tools. They're *prompts* to help you carry on an honest-to-goodness actual conversation with a stranger.

- *Are those pictures of your children? What do they want to be when they grow up?*
- *This is a beautiful house. I can see why you love it so much.*

- *Do you mind telling me a little bit about yourself, and I'll do the same? That way, it won't feel like this is some sort of awkward "first date."*
- *I know something dreadful must have happened if you're facing this terrible thing. Do you want to talk about it?*
- *Great collection of trophies! I'm a bowler, too. Which league do you belong to?*

How long you chat will usually depend on your part of the country. I'm from the South, and *small talk* is a way of life. It always starts out with "who are your people," meaning relatives. You're considered coarse, crude, and worse yet, probably a Yankee if you get straight to business during any meeting. On the other hand, my stepson lived up North for awhile, and reported to me that it was considered rude and inconsiderate to waste someone's time chatting instead of getting straight to the point. If you're not sure what direction to take, then feel your way gently. Also, resist smiling a lot. This is not a fun meeting.

It's vitally important to spend time getting to know the person you're dealing with. First, it's easier to have a good bedside manner if you think of people *as people* and not as customers, prospects, debtors, or something else equally impersonal. Second, when people are comfortable with you, they volunteer a lot more information you really need to know and might not think to ask. Third, if both of you relate to each other in a way that creates mutual trust and honesty, then the other person is much more likely to take your advice rather than foolishly resist.

Finally, you're coming upon someone at his or her lowest time, when feelings of vulnerability and loss of control are prevalent. It doesn't cost you anything to give back to them the dignity of a business relationship between equals. Equals generally have some things in common. Take the time to find that common ground.

Part of your job description as a Mortgage Workout Specialist is to remove anxiety and to restore respect. These things must be done in the very first meeting, and then nurtured in all subsequent meetings. If you're in a vastly superior position and take complete charge of the meeting, then you're helping to escalate anxiety.

Respect is usually recognized from your willingness to ask questions, *really* listen to the answers, and then engage in the normal ebb and flow of a true conversation. Engaging in a stilted interview, and making the other person wait patiently while you write down all their answers, is a sure sign of lack of respect. I'm not saying you shouldn't take notes or you should avoid looking at checklists. Just the reverse—I strongly recommend them, in fact. My point is that you should try to make the process as smooth and unobtrusive as possible, that's all. If an answer seems to invite another question, ask the other question. You're not being rude or nosy—you're showing that you pay attention.

If you're too nervous or inexperienced to pull that off, then be up-front about it. When it's time to get down to business, start with something like, "I know this is hard for you. It is for me, too, because I'm worried I won't do the right thing here. I need to ask you some questions before I can evaluate your situation and make recommendations. Would it be all right if I just read them from a list and get your answers?"

The goal is to put the other person in charge of the conversation as much as you can. Remember, selling is all about other people giving you permission to sell to them.

Make the Meeting a Success

In this first meeting, you will need to gain certain things. Every gain is a separate sale. This is what you need from that meeting:

◆ trust;

◆ information; and,

◆ a signed contract or a signed referral.

A signed referral is necessary when you decide you can't help someone, but you can refer them to another professional. I can't stress enough that people hear what they want to hear and they remember what they want to remember. High-stress situations like foreclosures result in some pretty strong self-delusional memories. It's extremely important that a property owner that you can't help know for sure that you won't be doing any work on his or her behalf. It might be equally important for you to be able to prove that you didn't hold out any false hope. Their signature, on a simple form advising of your inability to assist, but other avenues they should investigate, can prevent a lot of problems.

Trust

In order to get the things you need, you must earn the *trust* of the property owner. Trust can be built from many different sources.

Clothing will create a strong first impression. Some sales people will tell you to dress friendly in casual clothes, for example. That doesn't work here, because the owner has already received lots of worthless advice from friends. He or she needs an expert now. Like it or not, you have to look like an expert. Men—wear a conservative tie or a blazer—you don't need both. Women—slacks or moderate-length skirt and a jacket or cardigan sweater—nothing frilly, form-fitting, or revealing. Both of you, wear modest jewelry. You don't want to look like you're getting rich off other people's misfortunes.

Vocabulary is another major source of creating trust. You don't want to talk over someone's head, but you do want to use the right words for things. You might want to ask, early in the conversation, *Was your loan sold on the secondary market?* Most people won't have a clue what that means, so you get to explain it. The result—instant credibility.

Organization is important. Arrange your file before the meeting, and have at least two pens, in case one runs out of ink. Carry a notebook or legal pad with no other notes on it. You don't want someone seeing notes you made about other deals, and then wondering how much they can depend on your discretion in their case.

Insight:
Make sure your car is always neat and clean. If someone walks you to your car after a meeting, and sees it looks like a junk yard inside, then he or she will assume your mind is a junk yard. They will lose confidence in you.

Finally, honesty builds trust. Don't claim to know it all. Con artists have all the answers, not real people. If you don't know something, say so, but commit to find out within a specific period of time. In addition, if you don't know something, make a point of writing it down and then read the question back, so you make sure you're finding out the right thing. This also shows that you're a careful person. Once you find an answer, call back and tell the person the answer, or at least a progress report on getting the answer.

Honesty also means not sugarcoating why you're there. You need to be upfront with the person and tell him or her your intentions and abilities. The conversation may go something like what follows.

> If it's the right thing for the two of us, I'm interesting in buying your property before the bank takes it away from you. Then, I can rent it back to you for awhile and give you a chance to buy it from me when you get on your feet again. Or, if that doesn't work for us, I might rent or sell it to someone else. If I make a profit, I'll share that profit with you. If not, then at least you've preserved your credit rating and can buy something else in the future. If none of that seems possible, then I can recommend some other people who might be in a better position to help you. Does that seem fair enough for us to keep talking?

Put all of this in your own words, but make sure you cover each point. All of these tools will show that you're someone who can be trusted.

Information

After trust, you need *information*. I recommend using a form in order to get the facts you need. The one that follows should be used every time you conduct a first interview.

Date: _____   Property Address: _____

Person(s) being interviewed: _____
_____

Technically, who owns the property? _____

• • • • •

Name of Lender #1: _____
Address/Phone of Lender: _____

Account Number: _____ Monthly Pmt: _____

Approx date of loan: _____ Am't borrowed: _____

Loan Balance: _____ Accelerated? _____

Is foreclosure scheduled?_____ When: _____

Name and phone number of attorney for lender: _____
_____

• • • • •

Owner's estimate of value of property: _____

Estimate based on: _____
_____

Tell me what, exactly, you want to accomplish: _____
_____
_____

If there's more than one loan, use a separate form for each one. Fill out the "date" and "property address" at the top of each sheet of paper, and then the "loan" information in the middle.

You always want to ask the name of the legal owner of the property. I have a farm, for example, that's titled in the name of one of our corporations. If someone were interviewing me about my farm, they could spend all day in the real estate records and never find out any information because they'd be looking under *my* name. So, after all that wasted effort, they'd have to call me up, get the corporation's name, and then start over. Also, you might find out there are multiple owners and you need all of their signatures on a contract.

In the middle part of the form, the term "accelerated" might require some explanation. People usually refer to this as *calling the note*. There are three stages in the life of a real estate loan going bad. In the first stage, the borrower makes his or her payments on a regular basis. The second stage occurs when the borrower begins making payments late. If he or she gets past due, then the lender might let him or her stay behind, as long as he or she doesn't get over thirty or sixty days past due. At some point, the bank will demand that the loan be brought current. If that's not done, then the third stage starts, when the lender will declare a default and accelerate the note or make the whole thing due and payable immediately.

Many times borrowers will contact you *before* the note has been accelerated. They can see the train wreck ahead, but they're not there yet. These are your best opportunities to buy property at a reasonable price for no money down, and create a benefit for the owner.

You always want to ask the owner for an estimate of the value of the property. Usually it bears no relation to reality, but you need to ask, anyway. Suppose a house has a $90,000 mortgage on it, you think the property is worth $100,000, and the homeowner thinks it's worth $150,000. You've got a real uphill battle convincing the homeowner that the best he or she can hope for is avoiding all the bad consequences of foreclosure and maybe getting a *small share* of $10,000 when you sell the house. Or, maybe the best he or she can hope for is losing his or her equity, avoiding foreclosure, and being able to rent his or her own house back for a reasonable rent based on a $100,000 value, not a $150,000 value.

You never know, the owner might hit the nail right on the head regarding value. That's why you ask what he or she bases his or her opinion on. It might be that the house is in a subdivision of virtually identical homes. In the last three months, houses on this block have sold for $150,000 each. You're stunned, but he or she has the facts to back up the price. This information changes things. Now, this is a heck of a deal with many different ways to structure it.

Finally, ask what the borrower wants to accomplish. Do this *before* you start talking about different things *you* can do. You might be surprised how modest the homeowner's goals are. A borrower might be willing to abandon the property and the equity, if only you can *guarantee* you can stop a foreclosure, preserve his or her credit, and ensure there won't be a deficiency. This goal is extremely valuable to him or her—more valuable than a *possible* return of his or her equity—and it does not matter what you think your goal would be if in that same position. It is the homeowner's goals that you need to be listening to.

This is the hardest lesson for new investors to learn. Value is in the eyes of the recipient. If a property owner wants less for the property than you think is fair, then you have to remember the definition of *fair market value*. It's defined as *the price that a willing buyer would pay a willing seller with neither of them acting under duress*. A seller who wants or needs an immediate sale is under duress and willing to accept less than fair market value because time also has value to him or her.

I want you to internalize this—you are not cheating a seller who has placed a low dollar value on his or her property. Resist the urge to counsel him or her with your opinion of its worth. Resist the desire to show off how much you know and how well you can perform your own appraisals. If the owner's opinion of value is too high, then talk about that. If he or she wants little or nothing to get out of the mess, then simply write down what he or she wants and go on with your questions.

Those are the reasons for the items on the first interview form. You might need other information, depending on the circumstances. Some suggestions follow. Not everything will be relevant, so pick and choose. Don't just ask about the existence of things on the list; ask if they work. You'll still have to check, but most people are honest and will tell you the truth.

Residential

Lot size	Full/partial basement
Locate property corners	Water problems
House square footage	DSL
Name of builder	Cable
Slab, crawlspace, basement	Security system
Garage or carport, and number of cars	Security monitored by
Central HVAC	Lawn sprinklers
Gas systems	Elementary school
Number of bedrooms	Junior/Middle/High schools
Bonus rooms	Last year's real estate taxes
Dishwasher	Last year's school taxes
Garbage disposal	Other taxes
Septic or sewer	Restrictive covenants
Age of house and roof	Association dues
Age of electrical	Inside pets
Circuit breakers or fuses	Smokers in house
Age of plumbing	Date of last work on house
Age of pool	Other
Last time pool was serviced	

Commercial

Lot size	Lawn sprinklers
Locate property corners	Zoning
Building square footage	Tenants in place (leases)
Name of builder	Monthly rent, if full
Number of parking places	Monthly rent, now
Separate delivery entrance	Market rents
Central HVAC	Tenants pay any expenses
Gas systems	Tenants separately metered
Specialty appliances	Average monthly utility bills
Age of building	Highest monthly utility bills and when
Age of electrical	due
Circuit breaker or fuses	Anything changing (new roads, etc.)
Age of roof	Last year's taxes
Age of plumbing	Any inspections department notices
Phone system wiring	Any condemnation notices
DSL	Any special assessments
Cable	Association dues
Water problems	Restrictive covenants
Security system	Smoking/nonsmoking
	Date of last work on property
	Other

Most of the items on the lists have obvious importance, but I'll explain some of the more obscure ones.

♦ You want the owner to point out the property corners because the subdivision lot might not be as large as it seems.

Insight:
Learn about boundary line disputes early. In my experience, such disputes always end up in litigation, always go to trial, and always result in people spending $100,000 on legal fees fighting over $2,000 worth of land. If the amount of land in dispute is negligible, work something out or concede. Anything else is a waste of time and money.

♦ I like to know the name of the builder because I know which ones in town throw up junk that won't last more than six years.

♦ Pools need to be serviced every year, in my experience. If one hasn't been serviced in awhile, alarm bells should go off.

♦ Be aware that it's getting harder and harder to rent houses that can't secure high-speed Internet access—find out early if you'll be in a deprived area.

♦ Knowing the name of the security monitoring service can lead you to a source of information about false alarms, and about security in general.

♦ Unusually high utility bills could indicate a lack of insulation, an electrical problem, or an HVAC system going bad.

♦ You need to know the last time work was performed on the property because repair people can file what's called a mechanics and materialmen's lien. Usually, they can do this up to six months *after* the work was done. It operates like a mortgage that has to be paid, no matter who owns the property.

Sometimes you'll look at a residential property that can be converted to commercial. Be aware that, in many states, you'll have to pass a building inspection even if no construction or repairs take place. Simply because you've changed the use, you'll need to meet building code requirements for handicapped access, fire safety regulations, and perhaps other things. You may need more parking places, or perhaps you'll have to add shrubberies. You'll need to know what's already present before you visit the Inspections department to find out what they'll require.

Don't feel limited by this list. It's just my suggestions of things that are important. Add your own questions and rewrite the list as you gain more experience. Most people think business forms are things you buy, in bulk, at the office supply store and then use from now own. Experienced business people know that forms are living documents that change on a monthly or yearly basis, sometimes more often. I recommend that you put aside four hours, at least once a year, in order to revisit all your systems, procedures, and forms. Take a fresh look at them, like spring cleaning, and update them as necessary. You'll be glad you did.

Okay, you've gotten all the information you need, for now, from the property owner. With what you know at that point, do you think the owner's goal is reasonable? Sometimes a property owner won't be able or willing to tell you his or her goal. He or she will ask for your advice about what's possible. Here are the possibilities. Maybe more than one of them will apply. Never trot out the whole list. Pick the two alternatives you think are most likely, and discuss them.

- ◆ I buy your property, salvage some of your credit score, and maybe keep the bank from suing you for more money.
- ◆ I buy your property and rent it back to you.
- ◆ I buy your property, rent it to you, and give you a certain time limit to buy it back from me for an agreed upon price.

- I buy your property for the mortgage payoff and then pay you an agreed sum on top of that, in one year (or whatever time you need), but you get no money right now and you move out in _____ days.
- I buy your property for resale and we split the profits in a certain percentage.

If the goal is reasonable, then say something along the lines of:

> *Assuming there are no surprises, I think we can work something out along those lines. I'll need you to sign some forms, then I'll need _____ days to conduct my due diligence, and we'll meet again to evaluate what can be done.*

If you think the owner doesn't have a prayer of getting what he or she wants, but there's still a deal in there somewhere, then say:

> *With the little bit I know now, it doesn't seem possible to meet your goal. On the other hand, I'm willing to invest some time getting more information and trying to work out something creative that we can both be happy with. Do you want me to look into this some more?*

For those "I don't have a clue!" situations, you'll say:

> *This is a tough one and, frankly, I don't have a clue if we can do something together. Other people might TELL you they can fix things, but they're just being glib, telling you what you want to hear. Can you give me _____ days to get more information on my own, and then we can meet again to discuss this?*

Signed Documents

In all three situations, you need to get some forms signed. Here are the ones you'll need. (A sample real estate contract is in the Appendix.)

- ◆ Power of Attorney to Obtain Information
- ◆ Waiver of Confidentiality and Request for Information
- ◆ Real Estate Contract

The Power of Attorney to Obtain Information is necessary in case you have to sign something *in the borrower's name* in order to receive the information you need. The Waiver of Confidentiality and Request for Information allows his or her lenders to talk to you openly and freely. You'll have to leave a copy of the form with each lender for their files so you'll want to make several after they're signed. By far, the most important form is the Real Estate Contract.

Example: Your agreement with the borrower was that you would buy his house, sell it, and give him 10% of the profits. If it's not in writing, then he can go directly to the investor, agree to a sale on the same terms, and keep 100% of the profit. He already knows that the bank will accept less than the full payoff on the loan. Why does he need you at this point? He needs you if you have a signed, enforceable contract. It's as simple as that.

Please don't think this won't happen to you. Also, you can't pretend that only wicked, ruthless ingrates would do something like that to you. Some truly nice, ethical people will do exactly what I've described. They will tell themselves, and firmly believe, that you were only a vulture trying to cheat them out of their home. They will rationalize that they need the money more than you, and that you really didn't do all that much work, anyway.

I've found that people tend to take their commitments more seriously if they're in writing and signed. Plus, as I said earlier, most real estate contracts have to be in writing, anyway. They don't have to be notarized, though, so don't worry about that.

When You Can't Help

What happens if you can't help someone? Then, you need to get yourself out of there quickly and gracefully. If you spend all your time listening to the heartbreaking stories of people who can't benefit from your talents, then you'll never get anything done.

You'll know right away that there are some situations you just need to turn down. There's not enough time to do it properly, the numbers seem all wrong, or your belly is just telling you that you'll get hurt on this deal.

Never tell someone that you can't help them, unless you also offer them some other resource that can provide assistance. It's simple human decency. Plus, those same people, to whom you send business, will probably send business to you. Also, remember to get that signed referral form that's printed later in this chapter. Basically, it confirms that you will be taking no further action; you've given the property owner a list of other people who might be able to help, but you're not guaranteeing anything.

If you can't help, you should be in a position to recommend two bankruptcy lawyers, a legal aid society, two credit counselors, and two sub-prime lenders.

Sub-prime lenders make high risk loans. The very best, most credit-worthy borrowers are usually able to get loans at what's called prime interest rate. Subprime would seem to mean "less than prime rates," but the name is misleading. Actually, it means "credit scores way less than people who can borrow at prime, so the interest rate is way higher than prime." There are lenders who specialize in sub-prime loans.

Make a Recommendation

Whoever you recommend, your reputation rides on how good they are. If you do business in an ethical and compassionate manner, then you want to refer to people who have the same approach. Here's how you find those people.

There's probably only one legal aid society in town. Call them and obtain some brochures you can give out. Usually, the brochure will have the kinds of things the legal aid lawyers can and cannot do, and the restrictions regarding who's eligible. Also, make an appointment with one of the legal aid lawyers. Offer to bring doughnuts for the whole office, or just show up with the doughnuts. I'm serious. I always take $6 worth of hot Krispy Kreme doughnuts to the repair shop when my car needs work, for example. The mechanics remember me, they love me, my car gets fixed first! Not because I bought them off with a dozen doughnuts, but because I *thought about them* as people, not just robots who work on my car.

Once you're able to sit down with the lawyer, explain what you do. Say that you sometimes need to give people the names of other professionals who can help them. Your dilemma is that you don't want to send people to vultures. A legal aid lawyer will generally know the most ethical bankruptcy lawyers, the sub-prime lenders who aren't loan sharks, and the nonprofit credit counseling agencies. Usually, in the same conversation, the legal aid lawyer will give you the scoop about which ones to avoid like the plague. Besides getting valuable information, you will also be letting someone else know about your services—someone who might refer business to you.

As always, remember to write your thank-you note ahead of time and drop it in the closest mailbox after you leave the meeting.

If you don't have a legal aid society in town, then talk to a few ministers from the largest churches, and from churches in the less prosperous parts of town. They'll be able to make recommendations that are usually pretty much on the money.

After you get the names, visit the people you'll be recommending. You want to confirm they have the same values as you. It's also important to let them know you'll be referring business to them, and would appreciate it if they did the same. Leave some flyers with them—the same ones you gave to the bankers would be fine.

Ask them to let you know when someone you've referred uses their services. Not that you expect any fees, but you just want to know these people are in good hands. Keep track of this in a journal or on your computer. You want to review your notes periodically to see how your referrals are going. If you send eight people to John Smithson, a bankruptcy attorney, and he sends no one to you, then you need to pay John a visit. Point out all the business you've sent his way, and ask him if there are any opportunities for him to recommend *your* services to some of the people who contact him.

If there are three honest, ethical, and compassionate bankruptcy lawyers in town and one of them never refers any business to you, then quit sending clients to him. Switch to one of the others. On the other hand, sometimes there's really only one person who shares the same values you do. You can't refer people to someone, just because he or she will reciprocate. Do the right thing—continue to recommend the good lawyer. I always say, "What goes around, comes around." Your good deeds will come back to reward you, in some manner.

Avoid Hand-Holding

Once you've decided you can't help someone with your particular services, you can't afford to spend a lot of time in hand-holding. It might sound heartless, but it's not. The borrower has an urgent need to see someone who can provide assistance. It's foolish for both of you to continue talking when you obviously can't help. Rather than engaging in a long conversation about alternatives, I suggest you give someone the following form. Be sure to include names, addresses, phone numbers, and websites, if available.

Referral Advice

Thank you for your interest in my services. My specialty involves buying your property and negotiating with your lender in order to avoid additional charges or bad credit information. Some of my plans can also allow you to regain your property, or at least rent it for awhile until you find something better. Other plans anticipate selling your property in a fair way, instead of in a "fire sale." Sometimes I'm able to split profits.

For various reasons, I don't think I'll be able to implement any of these plans for you. Other caring and ethical professionals may be able to help you better. Below is a list of some people who have a reputation for honesty, integrity, and a sincere interest in their clients. Please feel free to mention my name when you call any of them.

Credit Counseling Services (Free): [Insert Name]

Credit Counseling Services (Fee based): [Insert Name]

Lenders Who Don't Require Perfect Credit: [Insert Name]

Bankruptcy Lawyers (Wage-earner protection, Chapter 13): [Insert Name]

Bankruptcy Lawyers (Business reorganization, Chapter 11): [Insert Name]

Have two copies of the form ready. Ask the person you've interviewed to sign one and give it back to you. Leave the other form with them. If they ask you why you want a signature, the answer is simple.

> *This is usually a very emotional time for people. It's not the best backdrop for a business discussion, and there's a danger of mistakes in communication. I like to get a signed copy of the form so I know that I've left one with you. Also, I worked really hard finding people who share the same values that I do. If you sign a copy of the form, then you're more likely to keep your own copy in a safe place, and have these names available for when you're ready.*

If a question ever comes up, the referral form is your evidence that you told someone you couldn't help them. In addition, though, you really want to make sure you always give it to people, and don't forget. It's valuable, free information. They should take advantage of it. Your explanation is absolutely truthful and accurate. It's just that you have *more* than one reason for getting the form signed.

● ● ● ● ●

That's about it for the first meeting with the property owner. By the end of the meeting, you should make one of the following decisions.

- ◆ Start working on a deal.
- ◆ Delay making a decision a certain number of days until you receive more information.
- ◆ Refer the borrower elsewhere.

What you don't do in this meeting is structure the deal. You've got too much research—due diligence—to conduct before you commit to a method of doing business.

11

Legal and Practical Due Diligence

After your initial screening to determine if the property interests you, your due diligence starts with the following questions.

- ◆ Exactly who owns the property?
- ◆ How many liens are there?
- ◆ What order are they in?

These are questions you must confirm the answers to. You can't simply ask someone. You must be sure the information you learn is correct. If you come up with bad answers to these questions, there's no point in conducting any other due diligence.

Priority of Liens

We say that a lien *attaches* to property when it becomes a legal obligation of the real estate. Most times, a lien attaches as soon as the mortgage is signed.

Priority of liens is an entirely different concept with different rules. Basically, priority determines who gets paid in what order (if there were not enough money to go around). A first lien gets paid first, a second lien gets paid second, and so on. Generally, we say that liens are either senior (better priority position) or junior (lower priority position) than other liens.

Here's the trick. Priority is determined by who records first, not by who gets a signed document first. A lien attaches when the mortgage is signed, so it's effective immediately between the borrower and the lender. Other people's rights aren't affected until it's recorded, though.

There are about a thousand ways someone can obtain a lien on property and have a higher priority than a supposedly first mortgage. It's pointless to go into any examples—it's like trying to give examples of snowflakes—no two are alike. You just need to know it's possible. Further, a foreclosing bank might be a second mortgage holder, so you must know the priority of the liens of the parties involved.

The first step to flushing out such problems is to ask the lender or the borrower. If either one tells you that the foreclosing bank is not in a first position, then stop everything. Rookie investors shouldn't try to negotiate a workout with more than one lender because it gets too complicated. Only the most sophisticated investors should buy at auction from anyone except a first lienholder.

If you have your heart set on buying a property from the second lienholder's auction, then obtain an *estoppel letter* from the first lienholder. A sample follows. In a nutshell, the first lender tells you how much its lien is and promises not to loan any more money or make any new claims under its documents. Having gone *on the record* and in writing to you, it can't deny it later. Estoppel letters are good in a variety of circumstances, any time you want to nail somebody down.

Sample Estoppel Letter

Bank Letterhead
Date
Internal Address

This letter will serve to confirm that, as of the date and time above, [Bank] has a first lien on certain real property described as _____ with a street address of _____ and owned by _____. The amount needed to secure a release of that lien is $_____. This number will be good until _____, after which the payoff will increase by _____ per day until paid in full. [Bank] affirms that it will not loan any additional sums to be secured by the lien, nor will it assert other claims under the security of the lien for the next _____ days.

Sincerely,

[Bank Officer]

If you can't follow my advice about not buying at second lienholder's auctions, then *be very careful*. I've heard the legends about someone paying $2,000 at a second lienholder's auction and then being able to assume a $100,000 mortgage on a property worth over $2 million. It has never happened to me, and don't hold your breath that it is going to happen to you. Getting greedy is the downfall of most new investors. Stay away from second lien foreclosures unless you're incredibly sophisticated *and* can afford to lose your money if it turns out badly. As I keep saying, if you can't afford to gamble; don't gamble.

Even if a lender tells you it has a first lien, do not take its word for it. While it is probably not lying, it might be misinformed. Mistaken information still has the same bad results as an outright lie. You'll have to check things out for yourself. You can personally do a lien search, which costs time, or you can buy a lien search, which costs money. You might be able to secure a copy of a title report from the foreclosing lender, so it never hurts to ask.

Buying a Lien Search

In most places, you can go to a *title insurance company*, also called a *title company*, and order a lien search. The fee's pretty low, but varies from place to place. In my experience, people are uncomfortable asking about the price of things ahead of time. The trick is to ask *before* you're ready to buy. In other words, don't wait until you need a lien search. Call several title companies as soon as you read this paragraph. Tell them you're putting together a budget, and you need to know how much it will cost to get a list of the owners and lienholders on a piece of property.

Most of the time they'll say something like, "Is this subdivision land or metes and bounds?" Tell them you're just putting together a budget, so you need both prices. Subdivision land usually has a description like "Lot 5, Block 10 of Enchanted Valley Estates." It's easier to research than metes and bounds land, which has a description that recites, "Start at the northwest corner of the southeast quarter of the southwest quarter of Section 19, Township 21, Range 12 West, thence turn an angle of 15 degrees 33 seconds west and proceed 185 feet... being 10 acres, more or less." These are harder to research because you have to read every single deed in the chain of title. For example, with a metes and bounds description, you might find a deed written twelve years earlier that goes through eighty-two lines of surveyor's lingo for a description and then, for the very first time ever, says, "Less and except the house and one acre of fenced yard I deeded to my Mom yesterday." Then, all the deeds afterwards never mention it again. This sort of thing happens all the time with metes and bounds descriptions, which is why you need to read every word of the deeds.

You should know that a *lien search* (also called a *title opinion*) is not the same thing as title insurance. Honest mistakes happen all the time, and for

your purposes, an opinion does nothing more than to disqualify certain properties. If a title opinion is wrong, you suffer the consequences. It usually contains some sort of language saying it's just an opinion, it might be mistaken,
and you're not entitled to rely on it. If the opinion is backed up by *title insurance*, the title company suffers the consequences.

Title Insurance

Title companies insure the *title* to real estate. Suppose, for example, you
wanted to buy a house for $50,000. You go to a title insurance company and
they check all the real estate records. Then they give you something called a
title binder. The binder reveals all liens against the property, plus the names of
all the owners. It also says that if you buy the property and pay off the liens,
the title company will guarantee there are no *other* liens, and no one except
the person named in the title binder owns the property.

Some of the things that are typically not covered by title insurance include
the following:

♦ things that only a survey would show, such as the fact that
part of your house is on your neighbor's land;

♦ claims of adverse possessors or squatters' rights. For example,
if there's a mistake about boundary line locations and a
neighbor has been keeping a garden, for twenty years, on
what's actually your land, then it becomes the neighbor's land
by virtue of adverse possession;

♦ forgeries, such as someone forging her husband's signature on
a deed;

♦ real estate instruments filed in the wrong place, so they don't
show up on a title search; and,

♦ whatever else they can think of.

Example: Let's suppose you obtain a title binder for property you want. It says Joe Jones owns the property in his name alone. First National Bank has a mortgage. It will take exactly $45,000 to pay off the mortgage note. There are no other liens.

Based on that, you close on the property at 4:30 on Thursday afternoon. You pay $50,000. Forty-five thousand dollars goes to First National Bank, and $5,000 goes to the seller, Joe Jones. But, at 4:28 that same day, while you were sitting in the reception area of the title company, someone recorded a judgment against Joe Jones, for $40,000. At 3:30 the next afternoon, the title company records your deed by filing it in the appropriate government office.

If a judgment gets recorded even minutes before your deed gets recorded, then it becomes a lien on your property. Without title insurance, *you* have to pay the additional $40,000 or the judgment creditor will foreclose on *you*! With title insurance, the title company just says, "Whoops! My mistake!" and they pay the $40,000 to the judgment creditor so you have the *clean title* they guaranteed you.

That "gets recorded" part is *critical*. Even if the property has already changed hands, all the money paid, all the documents signed, it's irrelevant if nothing's recorded. The first one to record, wins. In the trade, it's called *The Race to the Courthouse*. When you're buying foreclosure properties, then you're buying from someone who has financial problems. They probably aren't paying other bills, not just their mortgage company. It's almost always a "race to the courthouse" situation in foreclosures.

Here's the tricky part in title insurance—*the gap* between closing at, say, 4:30 on Thursday and recording at 3:30 on Friday. Some title companies insure you *as of the date, hour, and minute* the deed is signed and nothing after that. If the deed isn't recorded until a little bit later, then there's a gap when the seller no longer owns the property, but creditors can still file liens against the property. Always ask the title company if it insures the gap. Some do and some don't. Don't worry. You can shop for different title insurance companies just like you shop for the best deal on a car. Find one that insures the gap.

If the title company insures the gap, get it in writing. If they don't, and no one else in town will either, you can still protect yourself. Schedule your closing after the courthouse closes for the day, tell the title company you want to record your own deed, and then be at the courthouse when the doors open in the morning so you're the first person to record anything that day.

Add Owner's Coverage

Here's another secret about title insurance. Lenders always require title insurance, but it's for *their* benefit, not yours. You pay for the premium at closing, but only the lender is protected unless you do something extra. That extra is telling the title company that you want *owner's coverage* also. The additional premium is usually next to nothing.

Example: This is what happens if you just get lender's coverage and not owner's coverage. You buy a house for $100,000. The mortgage is $70,000, and you write a check for $30,000 for your equity. The title company issues title insurance *for the lender only*, in the amount of $70,000. You close on Friday afternoon and the deed is recorded first thing in the morning on Monday morning. Little did you realize that your seller was a con artist, though. He also sold the same property to someone else, across town, on Friday morning. They recorded their deed late Friday afternoon, as you were sitting at the closing table dreaming about your new home.

When you were forking over your $30,000, you were paying it to the wrong person, because he didn't own the property anymore! As a result, he had nothing to sell you, and you got nothing for $30,000. Of course, the crook also stole $70,000 from your bank, but *they* have title insurance. The title company pays the bank $70,000 on the bank's claim. You have no claim because you had no insurance. You're just out $30,000. It happens *all the time*.

Doing a Lien Search Yourself

You may get to the point that you feel comfortable doing your own lien searches. That's fine for disqualifying certain properties before you have to spend any money researching the deal. Plus, every sales contract should include a paragraph requiring title insurance. Another section should allow you to back out of the contract, without penalty, if the title insurance discloses new information that causes a problem for you.

However, auctions don't involve contracts. You show up, you bid, you win, you pay. Simple as that—no back doors, no loopholes. The information you put together before the auction is all you have to protect you once it is completed.

If you do your own title work in order to save money, then at least order a title opinion for the properties you want to bid on. You're not going to bid on everything you research, so you'll still be cutting expenses in noncritical areas.

In order to research title yourself, you need to know the following.

- ◆ Does the property have a Torrens certificate?
- ◆ Can you research real estate records online?
- ◆ Can you search real estate records by computer at the recording office?
- ◆ Where is the recording office?

Torrens Certificate

You'll remember from Chapter 8 that some states allow property owners to file a lawsuit and, at the end, obtain a certificate of title. From that point onward, everything affecting the title must be listed on the certificate. It's called a *Torrens certificate*. The Torrens system is not used everywhere, and may not be available in one part of a state but available in another. For those that do have it, you can look at the certificate itself and find out the names of all owners and all lienholders.

Always remember, a mistake can be made on the Torrens certificate, even if the chance is rare. Don't rely just on the Torrens certificate, but search the regular records also.

Real Estate Indexes

In order to understand researching title, you need to know how documents are filed and indexed. Real estate records are *indexed* so you can find things without having to flip through thousands of pages of deeds and things. Usually there's a *deed* index, a separate *mortgage* index, maybe a *judgments* index, and a *miscellaneous* index. An index is actually made up of many different volumes. There might be one book for 1970 to 1980, another one for 1981 to 1990, and so on. In addition, there would be one set of books called the *forward index* and another called the *reverse index*.

The forward index lists all the names of people who have *moved the ball forward* or taken some action that affected their piece of property. Usually, a person in a forward index sold the property to someone else or gave someone a mortgage on the property.

The index shows the name of the person who took the action to move the ball forward. That will be first. Then it shows the name of the person on the other side—the purchaser, or the lender, for example. Most importantly, it also tells you the book and page number where the actual deed or mortgage has been recorded. You go to another set of books, as directed in the index, and you can read the actual instrument.

The reverse index lists the names of people who *received* something having to do with real estate—usually they received a deed or a mortgage. Like the name suggests, you can use it to search backwards if the information you have allows you to go in that direction.

> **Insight:**
> Doing a title search using the index books on your own can be horribly complicated. I don't recommend it unless you're very experienced and have tons of time.

Computers make everything easier when they're available. You'll have to check with your local recording office to see if they are online, or if they have terminals at their offices. With a computer, you simply type in a person's name, tell the search engine that you want *all* records (forward, reverse, deed, mortgage, judgment, etc.) for all time periods. Make sure you find out how far back the computer records go, though. Sometimes only a few years' records are on the computer system, so you still have to do a paper search.

Find Out How Title is Held

Almost always, people own real estate outright, except for whatever liens are on it. Sometimes, though, property can be owned in different and sophisticated ways. For example, I can deed land to my brother *for and during his natural life* and then specify that it goes to my nephew. In this case, my brother has a *life estate*, and my nephew has the *remainder*. Either one of them can mortgage just his interest, and just that interest can get foreclosed on.

As another example, I could take some other land and give my sister a ninety-nine-year lease on it. (This is a pretty common arrangement for commercial property—it's called a *ground lease*.) For most people, a ninety-nine-year lease is pretty much the same as outright ownership. In my state, though, if my sister doesn't record something in the real estate records saying she has a ninety-nine-year lease, then it's good for only twenty years. Further, she could mortgage her *leasehold* interest, and the bank could foreclose on just the leasehold interest.

I could tell you about a lot more complicated arrangements, but they're way beyond the scope of this book. The point is, they're complicated. Avoid them, unless you really know what you're doing *and* you have a lawyer and a title company helping you. If you're doing your own title research, you'll have to read every last deed in the whole chain of title just to make sure that something weird didn't happen forty or fifty years ago.

What you need to look for and concentrate your potential purchase options on are the standard ways to hold title to real estate. They include the following with an example of how title might read.

◆ *Sole Ownership*: "Joe Jones"

◆ *Tenants in Common*: "Joe Jones and Marcie Jones, as tenants in common"; or maybe just, "Joe Jones and Marcie Jones." This means they own the property together, but neither one owns a particular *part* of the property. Either tenant in common can sell or mortgage just their share, or all of them can sell or mortgage the whole thing. If Marcie sold you her interest, then you and Joe Jones would be tenants in common. If Joe died, then his heirs (not you unless you are his heir) would get his interest.

◆ *Joint Tenants*: "Joe Jones and Bob Edwards as joint tenants with right of survivorship;" or maybe just, "Joe Jones and Bob Edwards as joint tenants." Joint tenancy means that they both own the property, just like tenants in common, but if one of them dies, the other one gets everything. A joint tenant can sell his or her share but the sale destroys the survivorship provisions making the new owners tenants in common.

◆ *Tenants by the Entireties*: "Joe Jones and Marcie Jones, as tenants by the entireties." About twenty-five states recognize this form of ownership. It's available only for husbands and wives. Like joint tenants whichever person dies first, the other one gets everything. If they own property as tenants by the entireties, then they both have to sign anything affecting the property or it's void. Neither one can sell their share all by themselves, and a divorce court can't order it out of one and into the other. Most importantly, creditors of one spouse can't seize the property. That is one reason this form of ownership has become so popular in some states. It serves as an asset protection tool.

If you see something on a deed that's not on the previous list, go see a lawyer or a title company, immediately.

Taxes

Many different taxing authorities might have claims against real estate even though they don't file liens in the real estate records. In most states, real estate (also called *ad valorem*) taxes and school taxes have a *super priority* in their liens. In other words, even though they come due year after year, long after other mortgages have been filed, the taxes still get paid first if there's a sale of the real estate. Also, the taxing authority has the power to sell the property at a foreclosure auction.

Tax assessors appraise property and then assess the taxes. The tax collector sends out the bills every year, collects the money, and forecloses if the bill's not paid. It used to be that tax collectors would let you ride for several years without paying your bill. It could grow to be quite huge. Maybe that's still true in some parts of the country, but in most places there's a cutoff date and, if the taxes aren't paid by then, the property gets auctioned. No excuses, no extensions, nothing.

To find out if any real estate or school taxes are due, you'll have to call or visit the tax collector's office in your county or parish. They'll need the property owner's name and the street address of the real estate.

While there, ask if there are any other government authorities who might have liens on the land. Visit those offices, too. They might be things like water and sewer board assessments, road improvement taxes, or lake-use taxes.

IRS Liens

The IRS and state/local governments can have liens, but they have to file in the real estate records, just like other creditors. Be aware that, if you find tax liens, it means any foreclosure has to have extra steps in it, or the government will still be able to take the property, even after an auction. Call your state revenue department, or whoever is in charge of local income taxes, and ask them what preforeclosure notices they require.

Under IRS rules and regulations, their lien continues, even after a foreclosure, unless they receive notice of the sale. Currently, the lender has to give the IRS written notice, by certified or registered mail, at least twenty-five days before the date of the auction. It has to be addressed to the *"District Director for the IRS"* in the district where the sale will be held and marked to the attention of the *"Chief, Special Procedures Staff."* The notice itself has to contain the name and address of the debtor, a copy of each Notice of Federal Tax Lien affecting the property, and a full description of the property being sold with the date, time, place, and terms of the sale. It also has to contain the approximate amount of the principal due and other costs and expenses of the foreclosure sale. If the lender postpones foreclosure, then the IRS is entitled to whatever additional notice is required under regular state law.

That's pretty technical. If the bank forgets to mark the notice to the attention of "Chief, Special Procedures Staff," then the IRS lien stays on the property. If you find IRS liens in your search, ask the lender for proof that they sent out the proper notices. Don't just take their word for it. If a banker gets offended, it's probably a good clue to pass on that deal and look elsewhere.

Other Tax Liens

Other taxes might show up in the real estate records as liens. These might be sales/use taxes, fuel taxes, occupancy taxes, or any number of things. You'll just have to call whoever has the lien and find out what their requirements are in case of foreclosure. I always write down the name of the person I talked to, and then read my notes back to them. *Then* I call back several hours later, ask for a supervisor, and ask the same question. You'd be surprised how often you get a different answer. Plus, without something in writing to verify the information they give, you will have no recourse from the governmental entity because you relied on what you were told over the phone.

Mechanics' and Materialmen's Liens

Repair people and contractors are generally protected under state laws. If they do work on your property and don't get paid, then they can file a lien against the real estate. Most times, they have up to six months *after* the work was done in order to file their lien. The best way to protect yourself is to ask the owner if they've made any repairs or improvements recently. Do it in a nonchalant kind of way. You might say, "I'm preparing my analysis of your property and what it's worth. Have you made any recent improvements or repairs that I should know about?" If they tell you about anything, then ask for copies of the cancelled checks, or ask if you can contact the person doing the work to make sure the bill was paid.

This is another good place to use an estoppel letter. Modify the one for a first lienholder. Put in the letter something saying that the repair person has been paid in full for the work. Include information indicating that any additional work in the next sixty days (or whatever you need) can't be done without telling you first.

You'll still need to get title insurance, just to be safe. The reason you ask about repairs and improvements early, though, is twofold. One, you might be able to cut a deal with the potential lienholder to take less money in order to help the sale of the property. Two, you might have a property owner who's difficult to deal with because he or she *thinks* that a repairman might file a lien against the property. If you find out that the work was completed nine months ago, but liens have to be filed in six months, then you know that the property is safe from that lien. As always, though, this stuff is tricky, so make sure you're on firm ground when giving advice and making decisions.

If you find out a supposed lien isn't effective, tell the property owner your opinion, and suggest he or she talk to an attorney. It's not ethical for you to take advantage of an unsophisticated seller by letting him or her *think* he or she has only $10,000 equity in his or her property when he or she might actually have $50,000. Don't give yourself a pep talk, either, and rationalize that the owner really owes $40,000 to a repair person and the lien status is irrelevant. He might have defenses to the $40,000 claim, if it ever came up in court. It's not your place to adjust the equities yourself so things work out to a result you think is fair. That's situational ethics, and it's wrong.

The third reason you ask about repairs and improvements is so you can find out quickly about problems that simply can't be fixed. If a house is worth $75,000, the mortgage is $70,000 and there's a potential mechanics' and materialmen's lien (usually called an M&M *lien*) of $35,000, then that's going to be an uphill struggle. You might or might not want to continue working on it.

Restrictive Covenants and Association Dues

It's becoming increasingly popular for subdivisions to have restrictive covenants in order to maintain the integrity of the neighborhood and keep the property values up. No one wants to pay $150,000 for a lot, build a $1 million house on it, only to have a neighbor build a metal shed to throw parties.

In order to prevent things like that from happening, many subdivisions have restrictive covenants. They'll say things such as, "any house has to have at least 3,000 square feet, a brick exterior, at least twenty feet of front lawn, and no boats, trailers, or motor homes parked within view of the street." If there are covenants, then usually every deed in the chain of title will recite that the property is subject to restrictive covenants, which can be found at a certain page in a certain book in the real estate records. That's why you have to read the deeds, not just look up the names in the indexes. You'll have to go read the actual covenants in order to find out what is and isn't allowed.

> **Insight:**
> Just because something's on the property now, doesn't mean it's allowed under applicable restrictive covenants or zoning. Sometimes violations are ignored until someone becomes angry and files a lawsuit. Other times, improprieties are *grandfathered*—allowed for the time being—but disallowed when the property changes hands.

Many times, if a neighborhood has restrictive covenants, it also has a neighborhood association that collects dues. The amount might be small, just enough to cover the annual Christmas party. Or, it could be huge. If the dues are delinquent, they could be a lien on the property, even though they're not recorded in the real estate records. That's because the paperwork that set up the association will be in the public records. From that, you're put on notice that you need to ask more questions.

Community Property States

You probably already know it if you live in a community property state, but to be sure, the following states follow community property rules.

- Arizona
- California
- Idaho
- Louisiana
- Nevada
- New Mexico
- Texas
- Washington
- Wisconsin

In those states, the husband and the wife must both sign all documents affecting property, even if the title is in just one of them.

If the borrower says they are married, then you know for sure. If they say they aren't, then you still need to check. You might find out from a credit report, but you'll have to get the person's permission to obtain the report. There might also be a central place in your state that you can call—a Department of Vital Statistics or something similar. If in doubt, ask someone at the place where marriage licenses get recorded in your area. They'll know if there's a central place to look up people's names in order to see if they're married or not.

Miscellaneous

There are other things you might need to check, depending on the circumstances. Here's a partial list.

Zoning

For whatever you want to use the property, you must make sure that it will be allowed under the zoning laws. Generally, this is no big deal with residential properties in residential neighborhoods. However, sometimes the zoning changes. Existing property might have been used in a non-conforming way, even though it's no longer legal in that zone. This is called *grandfathering*. For example, as a neighborhood builds up around a small commercial piece of property, the zoning of that property might change, but the store be allowed to still operate under the current owner. When the real estate changes hands, the grandfathering might disappear, and you won't be able to do the same things the former owner was doing.

Certificate of Occupancy

Inspections departments make sure that property complies with certain health and safety regulations. They can impact your life in two ways. After the purchase, any improvements over a certain dollar limit will require a building permit. That leads to an inspection, which can result in you being required to make other costly repairs having nothing to do with your original remodeling project. The second way is when you change the use of property from, for example, residential to commercial. It will require a new certificate of occupancy that can be withheld until you make expensive repairs or additions. Ask your local building inspections department about their rules.

Health Department

Many properties are not located on sewer lines—they have a septic tank that holds sewage until microbes can digest it. Local health departments are starting to crack down on old septic tanks, requiring them to be upgraded to newer, more expensive models. A change in ownership can trigger a health department inspection. Check with your local health department to find out their requirements.

Flood Plains

If the property you want is in a flood plain, then you'll have to buy flood insurance in order for a bank to loan you money to buy the property. You can always pay cash, and avoid the additional premium expense, but it's not a good idea to cut corners here. To find out if your property is in a flood plain, you can check with the US Corps of Engineers and ask to see their maps. In the alternative, talk to a real estate appraiser and ask if there are publicly available maps in your area. The maps change regularly. A lender might tell you that a property is not in a flood plain, according to their records, but things might have changed since the borrower bought the real estate.

School District

For residential properties, being in the right school district can make a tremendous difference. If it's important to you, or might be important to your tenants, find out where the district lines are. Even if you don't care, it can affect the resale value of a home.

Telecommunications

Is there fiber-to-the-curb, DSL, or cable television/modem for the property? These things are increasingly important to resale value and to rental rates.

Traffic Patterns

The traffic patterns affecting the property can make a big difference in the value of the property. For example, can you make a left turn onto a major road near the property during morning rush hour? Or, is the house located on a busy road that causes noise and safety problems? If you're looking at commercial property, can customers reach it easily? Are there any plans to widen or change roads, so that the traffic changes in the future?

Systems Inspections

A home inspector or an engineer can check out the property and tell you if it needs electrical work, roof repairs and other such things. As with any other profession, there are good inspectors and shoddy ones. Whoever you hire, ask for proof of liability insurance. If someone's offended; avoid them like the plague.

Utilities

You should always learn what utility companies service the property. Then find out if their bills have been paid and if there are any outstanding liens or assessments against the property. You should also try and learn if they are anticipating major rate hikes in the future.

Depending on your plans for the property, it may also be important to know if they have minimum fees that must be paid, whether you use the minimum levels or not. For rural property, find out if cell phone service, garbage pickup, and newspaper delivery are available.

Environmental Inspection

Even if your property never contained a dry cleaning plant, gas station, photo lab, or other source of hazardous chemicals, adjacent properties might have supported such businesses. The chemicals could have saturated all surrounding lands. Be sure to ask neighbors, especially the older ones, what the area used to be like and what businesses used to operate around there. It won't take the place of a full environmental inspection, but it'll give you a head start. If the property is a toxic waste site, you could be required to clean it up, even though you weren't the polluter.

Leases

Ask if there are any leases on the property. With residential properties, someone might have leased the basement to their mother-in-law for the next ten years, for example. That's an extreme example and something that probably would come up only with a crook. Most people are honest, but forgetful. Someone with a farm might have given a pasture lease to someone else for their cattle. A building owner might have rented someone else part of the parking lot. Find out exactly who you need to contact and who may have claims you must deal with if you purchase this property.

Adaptability to Another Use

I like to evaluate a business property based on whether it can be adapted to other uses. Even if there's a rock solid tenant in place, you just never know what's going to happen. A property that's a vanilla box, or easily changeable for a variety of purposes, is more desirable than a single-use building like a bank or car dealership. I won't reject a single-use building, but the adaptability factor impacts my estimate of the value of the property and the amount of risk I'm assuming if I buy it.

Eminent Domain Issues

Wouldn't it just be the pits if the highway department planned to widen a road, paid a homeowner for two-thirds of his or her front yard, and *then* the bank started foreclosure and you ended up buying the property? You'd be shocked to discover that you'd bought a house with no front yard. Check with government authorities and highway departments to make sure nothing like this is on the horizon.

State Statutes that Protect Consumers

More and more states are passing legislation that protects consumers in pre-foreclosure sales. Find out what your state's laws are, and comply with them.

12

Estimate Fair Market Value

air market value—usually written as *FMV*—is defined as the price a willing buyer would pay a willing seller with neither of them operating under any *duress*. Duress is some outside influence that affects people's judgment or decision-making. A pending foreclosure is duress because it depresses prices below what they would be under normal circumstances.

Sometimes duress can make people pay *more* money than a property's really worth. There's a tax loophole called a *1031 exchange*. It lets you sell one piece of property at a profit; put money in your pocket; buy another piece of property; and, pay no taxes. The trick is, you have to buy the second property in a very short time period. If you're running out of time, you're under duress. You'll spend more money than normal in order to buy something that qualifies under Section 1031. A buyer might be willing to spend $10,000 more than FMV in order to *save* $50,000 in taxes.

One way to estimate the FMV of a property is to look at sales of similar properties that sold recently. But, you need to do enough research to reject things that exchanged hands under some sort of duress. Duress could be situations like divorce, bankruptcy, or buy/sell agreements between partners.

In addition to duress, you can also get extreme prices when people sell property to their relatives or when they sell property to companies they own. (That last situation could go either way—high or low—depending on how the seller wants the sale to affect its books.)

> **Insight:**
> When examining recent property transactions, unusual sale prices should be considered with suspicion, no matter how much you want them to be true.

Calculate a Value

You may remember Jim from earlier chapters and the properties he is considering. In order to reach a rough estimate regarding fair market value of these properties, we'll use two systems similar to the ones used by real estate appraisers. The first is called the *comparables method* and the other is the *income approach*. The comparables system involves comparing different properties to each other in order to come up with fair market value. It's typically used for appraising houses. The income approach analyzes the value of a property based on the economic benefits enjoyed by an owner/investor.

Commercial properties are usually too diverse to use the comparables method, so you would use the income approach. Be aware that professional appraisers use three methods on commercial properties—comparables, income, and something called *depreciated replacement cost*—and then reconcile them. For us, that's more trouble than it's worth.

Researching House Values

Almost all large residential real estate companies have links on their websites to the local *Multiple Listing Service* (MLS). It's the database of homes currently being marketed by licensed real estate agents and by companies that offer fee-based MLS services to FSBO (For Sale By Owner, pronounced "Fizz Bow") sellers. You can search the database by school district, neighborhood, price limit, and other similar categories. If the service isn't available in your area, or you don't have access to the Internet, then pick up a *Showcase of Homes* or similar home sales magazine.

Jim did this, and learned his town had a wide variety of prices for three-bedroom, two-bath brick homes on small lots. He didn't find any for sale in Applecross, which was the subdivision with the foreclosure house he wanted to investigate. On the other hand, three-bedroom, two-bathroom houses in Polo Ridge sold for $150,000, and in Four Winds they sold for $100,000.

Why the difference? Lots of things can account for variances in value. Four Winds might consist of 30-year-old ranch-style houses of about 1,500 square feet. Polo Ridge could contain brand-new, 2,500 square foot homes with gourmet kitchens and swimming pools. As Jim did his general background research, he learned that houses in other parts of town seemed to sell for around the same prices as those in Four Winds. The same went for Polo Ridge. Jim was learning which subdivisions were comparable to each other.

After driving around the neighborhoods and talking to some real estate agents and lenders, Jim decided that Applecross—the location of the foreclosure house—was most similar to Four Winds. Because he couldn't find any recent home sales in Applecross to use as comparables, he could look at Four Winds, which did have several homes on the market. It was a starting point for his research.

Showcase of Homes and MLS services tell you what people are *asking* for their houses, not what they're actually *selling* them for. On the other hand, real estate agents generally know the market well enough to recommend an asking price fairly close to the FMV. If you find an asking price that seems out of the ordinary, view it with suspicion.

Use the form on the following page to gather information about properties that generally fit your purchase profile. Before long, you'll have an impressive bank of data you can use for comparables. By doing your homework and having the information ready at your fingertips, you'll be able to make the quick decisions sometimes required when buying foreclosure properties.

Profile of Comparable Homes

Date: _____ Property Address: _____

Name of Subdivision/Area of Town: _____

Question	Answer	Notes
Asking price		
Actual sales price		
Approximate square feet		
Lot/Land size		
Age of house		
Age of roof		
Exterior: brick, wood, etc.		
Number of bedrooms		
Number of bathrooms		
Garage/carport/nothing		[Be sure to include number of cars.]
Sewer or septic tank		
Fireplace		
Elementary School		
Middle/Junior High School		
High School		
Average commute time		[Estimate to the place where most people work.]
Condition: good/fair/poor		
Other:		
Other:		

Real estate agents with access to the full MLS database can generally find out the actual selling prices of property. That's because they share the information with each other, via MLS, as their properties go to the closing table. Without that access, you'll have to work a little bit harder.

If your local real estate records are online, that's the easiest way to get the information. Sometimes the recording office will show the sale price on the face of the document, or in the notes. Another possibility is to check with the property tax assessor's office—it might have the information you need. Usually, when a piece of property is purchased or a claim to a homestead exemption filed, the assessor asks how much was paid for the property. Other times you'll have to look at the recording fee information and figure it out. This varies from state to state, and sometimes among counties within a state.

In my county, for example, sale prices are not revealed on the face of the deed or in the online notes. I can see the deed taxes, though, and figure out the sales price from there. Whoever records a deed has to pay a recording tax of $1 per $1,000 of equity in a property. If a $100,000 house is purchased for $30,000 down with a $70,000 mortgage, then the recording tax will be $30. If I see a recording tax of $30, I know that there is $30,000 worth of equity in the property.

Next, in my county, I can look at the mortgage records. Mortgages always say the mortgage amount. Add the two numbers together—the equity and the mortgage—and you know what the house sold for. You should be able to figure out how to work backwards from the forms and taxes that are recorded in your area in a similar way.

Jim's problem was that Applecross was a small subdivision without any sales within the past five years. He had to look at sales in other subdivisions that were similar to Applecross. That's where his general research came in handy—he knew that Four Winds was very similar to Applecross.

According to Jim's research, there had been three house sales in Four Winds in the past two years. He consolidated their information, using a variation on the Profile of Comparable Homes, introduced earlier in this chapter. He also included the information for the house in Applecross. The form on the following page is very similar to the ones used by professional appraisers.

Comparable Home Sales Analysis

Date: _____

Comparable #1 address: _____

Comparable #2 address: _____

Comparable #3 address: _____

Subject [Applecross] address: _____

Question	#1	#2	#3	Applecross
Asking price				
Actual sales price	109,000	90,000	85,000	
Approximate square feet	3,000	2,500	2,500	2,500
Lot/Land size	? acre	? acre	? acre	? acre
Age of house	30	30	30	30
Age of roof	new	10	15	10
Exterior: brick, wood, etc.	Brick	Brick	Brick	Brick
Number of bedrooms	4	3	3	3
Number of bathrooms	3	3	2	2
Garage/carport/nothing	2-car	2-car	Carport	2-car
Sewer or septic tank	Sewer	Sewer	Sewer	Sewer
Fireplace	No	No	No	No
Elementary School	Vestavia	Vestavia	Vestavia	Prewitt
Middle/Junior High School	Grissom	Grissom	Grissom	Grissom
High School	Roberts	Roberts	Roberts	Roberts
Average commute time	15 min.	15 min.	15 min.	15 min.
Condition: good/fair/poor	Excellent	Good	Poor	Poor
Other:				
Other:				

After looking at all the comparables, Jim saw there wasn't an exact match for his Applecross House. Comparable #3 seems to be closest, but it had a carport. Jim's property had a two-car garage. At this point, he had to make an estimate regarding how much a garage would add to the value of a house. This was just a guess, but it's the same system professional appraisers use.

Comparable #3 is a thirty-year-old house in poor condition. A potential buyer would probably be on a very modest budget. A garage doesn't generally add much monetary value to that demographic group. A price-conscious person couldn't afford to pay more money for something considered a luxury. Jim's estimated that such a buyer might pay $1,000 extra to buy the identical house, but with a garage. He's going to add $1,000 to the sales price of $85,000, and arrive at $86,000. This should be fairly close to what his house in Applecross would be worth.

You'll have to develop your own system for what features add or subtract value from a house, and how much that value is. There are no hard and fast rules. In a neighborhood of starter homes, a garage won't add a lot of value, because the market place of buyers simply can't afford to pay much more. The pool of potential buyers for a starter home will probably gladly sacrifice a garage in order to save money on their monthly payments.

On the other hand, in an *upper bracket* area (upper middle class but not rich), people demand a two- or three-car garage. The lack of a garage probably depresses values as much as $50,000, because anybody buying a house in this type of area will immediately build a garage.

When analyzing comparables, don't think about how much it would cost to duplicate a particular feature or amenity. What's important is how much that item would add to the value, and prompt a buyer to pay a little bit more in order to get it. In starter homes, a swimming pool doesn't add much value, and might actually depress the price because of the economic burden of keeping up the pool. For more expensive homes, it might add significantly. An extra bathroom or bedroom always seems to be valuable. School zones are critical for most residential properties, and can significantly alter what someone will pay for a house.

Insight:

Comparing selling prices of houses rests on an assumption that the owner is going to live in them. Unless a neighborhood is in decline, an owner/occupier will, almost always, pay a slightly higher price than an investor looking for rental properties. Declining neighborhoods usually convert to higher levels of rental homes as owners move out, but keep their houses for leasehold income. Investors are attracted to those areas as they try to buy multiple properties in order to gain economies of scale for expenses and management.

Income Approach

If you're buying a house to resell or to live in yourself, then use the comparables method to arrive at a value. If you're buying a house so you can rent it out, then you *also* need to use the income approach in order to get an accurate feel for the value.

The income approach assumes a property *will* be rented out, even if it's currently being used by the owner. Rents are calculated as an amount per square foot. Sometimes that's expressed in annual terms, sometimes per month. The post office Jim considered rents for $1,000 per month and has 2,000 square feet. That's $1,000 (monthly rent) divided by 2,000 (feet) to give you $0.50 *rent* per *foot* per month. Most of the country calculates rent on an annual basis. In our example, $1,000 per month rent, times twelve months, equals $12,000 per year. $12,000 rent, divided by 2,000 feet, gives you $6 rent per foot per year. Whenever someone quotes you a rental rate, be sure to ask them if it's monthly or annually.

With commercial properties, you always need to know what the rent *includes*. Sometimes the tenant pays a simple rent and the landlord pays all the expenses like taxes, insurance, utilities, parking lot maintenance, and other things. Sometimes the tenant has to pay some or all of these expenses on top of his or her monthly rent. If a tenant pays all the expenses associated with the property, it is called a *triple net lease*. If the tenant pays only some, it's called a *net lease* or a *net-net lease*, and you have to ask *which* expenses are borne by the tenant.

At first glance, all of Jim's potential purchases seem equal, because they all generate $1,000 a month in gross rent. This can be misleading, though, because of variations in who pays for the property expenses.

Take a look at of the post office building and the chiropractor's office, and an estimate of a rental scenario for the house. Under their respective leases, the landlord pays more of the expenses for the post office than he or she does for the chiropractor's office. The chiropractor is required to pay the insurance premium for the building and the janitorial and lawn care. A residential tenant typically does not pay any of the property expenses.

The *Comparing NOI of Investment Properties* form will help you focus on how much of the gross rent can expect to find its way into your pocket.

Comparing NOI of Investment Properties

	Post Office	**House**	**Chiropractor**
Annual Rent	+12,000	+12,000	+12,000
Insurance	-500	-400	0
Real estate taxes	-1,000	-400	-1,000
Janitorial and/or repairs	-250	-100	0
Lawn care	-250	0	0
Net Operating Income	=$10,000	=$10,000	=$11,000

Figuring out the fair market *rent* for similar properties, with similar expense allocations between landlord and tenant, is the first step in your analysis. You do this even though your property already has a tenant, because the *tenant* might be paying less than *market* rent. There are many reasons an investor might have a tenant at below-market rents. The following is a list of the most common reasons for below-market rents.

◆ The landlord fears that raising the rent will cause a tenant to leave. This can be avoided by putting annual rent escalations into your lease. That way, rent increases are automatic, and they're usually a relatively small amount each year.

◆ The tenant performs some responsibilities, such as fixing up a house, in return for decreased rent.

◆ The tenant works for the landlord in some other business, so the landlord has given the tenant a discount on the rent in return for cheaper wages.

◆ The landlord simply has not kept up with market rents in the area, and doesn't know how much to charge.

◆ With larger, commercial properties, a tenant might have below-market rent because the landlord didn't have to pay a leasing commission or any fixup expenses in order to obtain the tenant. A savvy tenant can negotiate those expense savings into a smaller rent payment.

You shouldn't base your calculations on the rent actually being received by the former owner, unless you intend to keep the same tenant in place at no rent increase.

After you learn what market rents are for similar properties, you multiply that figure by however many square feet are in *your* property. If market rents are $6 per foot, and your property has 1,200 square feet, then you'd multiply $6 times 1,200 feet to get $7,200 per year or $600 per month.

Some people stop at this point and use a *rule of thumb* to calculate the value. They say a property is worth 100 times its monthly rent. This is called the *gross rent multiplier*. If the monthly rent is $600, then you multiply that by 100 and get a fair market value of $60,000.

> ### Insight:
> In my experience, the full income approach analysis usually yields a value a little bit higher than the gross rent multiplier method. Since most people value their own property using the gross rent multiplier, then they might have a lower opinion of the value than is realistic. You're under no obligation to educate people about different valuation methods. Just be aware that appraisers use the income approach; bankers loan money based on the income approach; and, the majority of investors buy based on the income approach. If you buy based on gross rent multiplier and you sell based on the full income approach, then you're usually buying low and selling high.

I recommend using the gross rent multiplier to *disqualify* properties. If market rents are $600 per month, but a seller is asking $120,000 for his or her property, that's 200 times the monthly rent instead of 100 times. I don't need to do a full economic analysis to figure out that the price is too high!

The income approach analysis starts with the gross annual rents—how much money would the property bring in if it were fully rented out for an entire year at market rents. That's your *gross income*. Next you need to determine your annual expenses. These are things like real estate taxes, insurance, and maintenance. They might also include utilities, garbage pickup, and management fees. If the tenant pays for certain expenses, then they aren't *your* expenses.

Depending on the size and type of the property, you might need to estimate an expense for vacancies and bad debts. Jim's Post Office, with a twenty-five-year lease to the United States government, will not have any vacancies in the foreseeable future. The chiropractor's office won't have any in the next two years, but the rental house could be vacant for at least one month. You would allocate a vacancy expense equal to one month's rent for the rental house.

After subtracting all the expenses of *operation*—which don't include mortgage payments—you obtain the *net operating income* (NOI). In case it's starting to get a little confusing about when you subtract mortgage payments for your calculations, here are the rules.

NOI is net *operating* income—the money left after subtracting the expenses *any* investor, including those paying cash and those with 100% financing, would have to pay each year. NOI calculations do not include any amount for financing, even if it's present.

Cash flow calculates how much money you can spend at the end of the year. You add all your income, and you subtract everything for which you have to write checks, including the full mortgage payment.

Profit generally has to do with income taxes. You add all your income and you subtract all your deductible expenses in order to arrive at profit. Mortgage interest is deductible. Repayment of principal is not. As a result, only a portion of your mortgage payment is deducted as an expense. In addition, you can deduct depreciation each month, even though it's not something for which you have to write checks.

Net operating income is like the holy grail for investors. Sophisticated investors always talk in terms of NOI. Unsophisticated investors (successful or not) usually don't know what it means. Don't assume someone is naïve just because they don't know what you're talking about when you ask them what the NOI is on their property. You can never go wrong talking to someone about NOI and then dropping back to *gross rent multiplier*, if they don't understand you.

The Cap Rate

Once you know the NOI, you can perform some calculations to arrive at a probable value. To get from NOI to value, you have to use a tool called the *cap rate*, which is short for *capitalization rate*. (Nobody uses the full phrase, just the short version.)

Cap rates are easy to understand if you realize they are a fictional substitute for interest you could earn on a hypothetical investment. For example, if you had cash to put in a bank account and wanted to earn $200,000 per year, how much money would you have to deposit? To answer that question, you'd have to know how much the bank is paying in interest. At a 3% interest rate, you'd have to invest or deposit (essentially *spend*) a little over $6.6 million in order to earn $200,000 per year.

What if you didn't have that much money, but still wanted to earn $200,000 a year? You might loan money to people with bad credit. There's a lot of risk, so you might charge them 20% interest. To figure how much you now need to spend in this situation, you take the $200,000 you want to earn and divide it by 0.20 (20% is 0.20) to get $1,000,000. One million dollars, loaned out at 20% interest rates, will earn you $200,000 a year. You can spend a smaller amount of money to earn the same income every year, but that income is riskier and less reliable.

Investment real estate works the same way. There are no hard and fast rules about cap rates. Just like interest, if the deal is risky, you want a higher return on your investment. In the investing world, risk is related to two things—what's the risk you might not get your rent payments in a timely manner and, secondly, what's the risk that the market for your property is so unique that it might take a long time to find a buyer or a new tenant. An established car dealership might be a risk-free investment as far as monthly rent. If the lease expires, though, and the tenant moves to a newer part of town, your property's probably going to stay vacant a long time while you search for a new tenant. This property is somewhat risky, even though the current tenant is not.

One of Jim's foreclosure purchase opportunities was the Post Office building. If it had twenty-five years left on the lease to the United States government, and the NOI was $10,000 a year with annual rent escalations to keep up with inflation, then this would be a solid gold, reliable, income stream. Jim might be willing to earn only 5% per year on his investment money needed to buy the post office. To find the value that meets Jim's criteria, he divides the $10,000 NOI by the cap rate of 0.05 and obtain a figure of $200,000.

Another property Jim is examining is the small rental house. It has more risk associated with it because he might not be able to keep it rented 100% of the time, and because a tenant might cause damages requiring expensive repairs. In order to justify investing in this property, Jim might want a higher return on his money.

Insight:

You can generally discover market cap rates for particular types of commercial properties, such as apartments, office buildings, and post offices, by asking real estate brokers or commercial lenders. Single-family, residential properties, however, generally don't have widely recognized cap rates because they are usually the province of smaller investors with more diverse properties. In order to complete a cap rate analysis, you'll have to pick a rate that you're comfortable earning on your money.

Jim might want to earn 12% on his money in order to justify buying the rental house. At an NOI of $10,000 per year, Jim could afford to spend no more than $83,000 to buy the house. If the borrower owes $85,000, this is going to be a tough sales job, and will have to involve the lender agreeing to accept less than full payoff for the loan.

The cap rates change periodically, depending on market forces. If a large university announces that it's going to build five new dorms, then you might see cap rates for student apartments in that part of town climb to 8%, because vacancies will go up when students move out of apartments and into dorm rooms. When the announcement comes out a week later that the university is going to demolish five old dorms, then people will realize that vacancies will not increase after all. Cap rates will go back down again. Remember, a higher cap rate means higher risk. More risk means you're not willing to pay as much to buy that investment. Higher cap rates translate to lower values.

Fixing Up the Property

The other way cap rates come into play is in figuring out how much more valuable a property will become if you buy it and fix it up. If the rental house could be improved somewhat and the rent increased, what would that do to its value?

Jim might decide that he can install a washer/dryer in the rental house for $600; do a little landscaping for $200; paint the interior for $400; replace all the carpet for $1,000; and, fence the back yard for another $1,000. That's total expenses of $3,200. Afterwards, he can charge $1,200 per month in rent instead of the $1,000 the current owner is charging. Jim will now have $14,400 in gross annual income, $2,000 of expenses, and a resulting NOI of $12,400.

Jim assumes, because he's done some research, that most rental house investors *in his area* want to earn 12% on their money, meaning they'll buy at a cap rate of 12%. Dividing the NOI of $12,400 by a cap rate of 12% (0.12), we get a value of $103,333.

Jim can buy this property for the $85,000 mortgage payoff and then spend another $3,200 fixing up the property in order to justify higher rents. *Now*, he's looking at being able to buy a $103,333 property for just $88,200. *Before*, he was faced with needing to spend $85,000 to buy a property worth $83,000. Here's a comparison of the before-and-after valuation process for the house.

Insight:

If you have a credible plan to improve real estate through repairs and minor upgrades, and then sell it within one year for at least 20% more than the total of your purchase price and repair expenses, you can generally borrow 100% of the money you need.

Comparing Investment Property Values After Rehab

	Before	After
Gross income	+12,000	+14,400
Vacancy losses	-1,000	-1,000
Insurance	-400	-400
Real estate taxes	-400	-400
Janitorial and/or repairs	-100	-100
Lawn care	0	0
Net operating income	=$10,000	=$12,400
Cap rate	12%	12%
Value	$83,000	$103,000
Value added by improvements		+20,000
Money needed to add value		$3,200

Is this a good investment? Sure it is! Jim can use his superior knowledge and experience to work with the owner to avoid foreclosure, preserve him or her credit rating and self-esteem, and put $15,300 in his pocket when he sells the property.

Estimating the value of the chiropractor's office could be a little trickier. If Jim is going to maintain the status quo, then he would do a simple income approach analysis to arrive at a value. On the other hand, the property contains about 2.75 acres of surplus land that could be developed. Jim would then use the income approach to value the building and ¼ acre of land. He'd use the comparables approach to value the 2.75 acres of land, and then he'd add the two numbers together. After a purchase, Jim could build more offices or he could just sell off the surplus land and pocket that money as profit.

13

Rental Properties and Cash Flow

In order to understand cash flow, you should imagine your piece of real estate has its very own checking account. All the income (rents, late fees, etc.) goes into the account. All the things for which you have to write checks—mortgage payments, utilities, taxes, maintenance, etc.—are written out of the checking account each year. In our example, you must write checks for *all* bills. You're not allowed to get past due on a bill and hope to have enough money next year to pay it. For purposes of cash flow analysis, you write all the imaginary checks even if there's no money in the bank.

After you've made all the deposits and written all the checks, you'll either have money left in the account at year-end, or you'll be overdrawn. If you have to put extra money in the account to prevent checks from bouncing, then your investment has a *negative cash flow* for that particular year. In other words, before you make those extra deposits, the balance in your checking account is *negative*.

The next year, on January 1, you start all over again with a "0" balance in your account. For purposes of cash flow, each year is evaluated by itself.

If you don't have to make extra deposits but, instead, you have money left in the account at the end of the year, then your property has a *positive cash flow*. You might also say, "My investment is cash flowing."

On Paper

Something can be profitable and still have a negative cash flow. In other words, it can be profitable *on paper*, but put you in bankruptcy at the same time, because there's not enough money to pay the bills.

By the same token, something can be *unprofitable*, but still have a positive cash flow. This situation is a lot better than it sounds. It means you put money in your pocket every year, but you don't pay any taxes because, *on paper*, you're going broke. That's usually possible only with large depreciation deductions such as you get from convenience stores or from something called *category depreciation* on new construction. Don't waste your time looking for properties with positive cash flow, but paper losses. They're rare and tricky.

Profit vs. Cash Flow

The more common instance you'll encounter is someone telling you a property is profitable and then you learn it has a negative cash flow. Let's say a banker tips you off about a foreclosure coming up. It's a small trailer park—almost management free and *highly profitable* according to the banker. He tells you the owner is in trouble because of some gambling debts, not because of this particular investment. Total rental income is $4,000 per month and the profits are $500 per month. You can buy this property at foreclosure, the bank will finance 100% of the purchase price, and everyone will live happily ever after. Or will they?

To an accountant and most investors, *profit* has to do with IRS reporting and internal bookkeeping. *Cash flow* has to do with being able to put spending money in your pocket. You can take cash flow to the grocery store. Profit is a number on a piece of paper.

The trailer park might bear closer scrutiny. Suppose it consists of lots or *pads*. Tenants bring in their own mobile homes. Rental income is $4,000 a month. The expenses consist of real estate taxes, street repair, outdoor lighting, liability insurance, legal and accounting, and mortgage interest. That adds up to $3,500 a month. The project makes a profit of $500 per month.

Rental income	+4,000
Real estate tax expense	–700
Insurance expense	–500
Outdoor lighting	–200
Legal and accounting	–400
Street maintenance	–600
Mortgage interest	–1,100
Profit	$500

While this looks incredibly rosy, the banker neglected to mention that mortgage payments consist of more than just the interest. You also have to pay something on the principal. Payments to principal are not expenses for accounting purposes, so they're invisible when talking about profit and loss. Unfortunately, they sure demand the limelight when you have to write checks for them.

As a beginning investor, cash flow is probably more important to you than profit. I'm assuming you want to buy foreclosures in order to supplement your income. Here's what your cash flow would look like for the same property.

Rental income	+4,000
Real estate tax expense	–700
Insurance expense	–500
Outdoor lighting	–200
Legal and accounting	–400
Street maintenance	–600
Mortgage interest	–1,100
Mortgage principal reductions	–600
Profit	–$100

That's right. The exact same property has a $500 per month profit, but a $100 per month negative cash flow. You have to take $100 a month out of your regular paycheck in order to pay all the bills on this investment. A person could go broke pretty quickly with such a good investment. In fact, a person could end up in foreclosure.

Insight:

In the investment, there is nothing unethical, illegal, or dishonest about saying a property is profitable even though it has a negative cash flow.

NOI and Cash Flow

If you plan to rent your property out, then you'd do an NOI analysis (see Chapter 12), but you'd include an extra line for the mortgage payments. That lets you know what your cash flow will be.

Let's look at the three properties Jim is reviewing. Assume he'll have to spend $200,000 to buy the post office building because that's the probable value and there's a large national market willing to spend that amount. He'll have to make a 20% down payment to obtain financing. Assuming he can buy the rental house for the $85,000 mortgage payoff, he can obtain a loan for the full purchase price, plus repairs, or $88,200. Finally, assume the chiropractor's office can be purchased for the $85,000 loan payoff, but it has a value of $120,000 because the excess land can be developed or sold. Jim can probably get a line of credit to buy the chiropractor's office and build more offices, but he's just going to borrow $85,000 in the beginning.

The post office will be set up on a traditional 30-year mortgage at 6% interest. If Jim intends to fix up the rental house to resell, and he plans to develop the chiropractor's property, then he can probably obtain an interest-only loan for the first year, at the same 6% interest.

The cash flow analysis for all three properties follows.

	Post Office	Chiropractor	House
Gross Annual Rents	+12,000	+12,000	+12,000
Potential Vacancies	-0	-0	-1,000
Landlord Expenses	-2,000	-1,000	-1,000
Net Operating Income	=10,000	=11,000	=10,000
Annual Mortgage Payments	-11,511	-5,292	-5,100
Annual Cash Flow	-$1,511	$5,708	$4,900

As terrific as the post office investment is, Jim might not be able to afford it because of the negative cash flow in the early years. On the other hand, if he wants a nest egg for the future, and can afford negative cash flow for awhile, the post office is a good place to invest his money.

For the typical foreclosure investor, though, the rental house will be the best investment. That's because it can generate almost $500 a month while you are holding it, and you can sell it for a $15,000 profit. The chiropractor's office is riskier if you want to sell, because your profit has to come from building new offices or from breaking off the surplus land and selling it separately. If you want to buy a foreclosure for the steady rental income, then the chiropractor's office will need a traditional 30-year mortgage, which reduces your annual cash flow to around $3,500.

Evaluate Using Cash Flow

At first, the Post Office seemed to be the best purchase for Jim—it had a solid tenant on a long-term lease at market rents. On further analysis, though, Jim might have second thoughts. The rental house produces immediate cash flow, which is always nice. That might not be so important to Jim, who knows his job is secure for another year. He might be willing to have negative cash flow in the first year in order to get the reliable income and an easily marketable property should he want to sell.

The point is, you can't take other peoples advice about profitability—because they use the term loosely—and you can't go with your gut instincts. You have to use the analytical tools I'm giving you in this book *and* do your due diligence.

14

Additional Costs to Factor into Your Planning

It's always more fun to talk about income than expenses. Expenses are like speed traps, though—unpleasant consequences if you're surprised, but manageable with a little warning. This chapter alerts you to a wide variety of *speed traps* that need to be programmed into your investing *radar detector*.

Property Acquisition Expenses

Surprises at the closing table probably account for more heart attacks than greasy hamburgers and fried chicken. By law, the closing agent is supposed to let you know, at least twenty-four hours in advance, how much the closing expenses will be. In addition, most state agencies that license real estate agents require an agent to give you a good faith estimate of closing costs as soon as you make an offer on a property. In the real world, these things rarely happen. You need to know how to do the calculations yourself. The Department of Housing and Urban Development (HUD) has a form called a HUD-1 (pronounced "hud one"—don't spell out the initials) that's supposed to be used by residential lenders to itemize all closing expenses.

> **Insight:**
> Single-family, residential properties always have a HUD-1 at closing. Commercial properties might have a HUD-1 or a Settlement Statement depending on what the closing company is comfortable with, but the investor *always* refers to the document as a Settlement Statement. (Investors who talk about HUD-1's are perceived as amateurs.)

Many times, a commercial transaction is too complicated to fit into the preprinted items on a HUD-1, so that's the reason for a separate Settlement Statement. Because the HUD-1 is always printed on a legal size piece of paper, a sample is not provided. However, you can find the form, and a really good explanation of what goes in the blanks, on the Internet at **www.hudclips.org**. You can also go to any mortgage company or title company and ask for a blank copy.

Closing Costs

Everybody can figure out that the down payment on a $100,000 house is probably going to be 20%, or $20,000. It's the closing costs that make life tricky and expensive. Here are some of the most common ones.

Attorney's Fees, Document Preparation Fees, and Title Company Closing Fees

Most times the attorney's fees, document preparation fees, and title company closing fees will be a set amount unless there's something pretty complicated about your transaction. Call around to the title companies and ask them what these expenses typically run in your area. Usually, buyer and seller split these expenses equally. In a preforeclosure situation, though, the seller usually can't afford to split, so you end up paying 100% of this expense. (There are no hard and fast rules about who pays what.)

Recordation Fees

Recordation fees are what you pay your local government in order to record the deed and any mortgage. In the typical real estate sales contract, the buyer pays recordation fees. Call your local recording office and ask them what all their fees are for deeds and mortgages. If you don't ask for a complete rundown of recording expenses, they'll sometimes tell you it's $5 for the first page and $2 for each additional page. They won't think to volunteer that you *also* have to pay a certain amount per $1,000 of equity, another amount per $1,000 of mortgage loan, indexing fees, or other things.

Tax and Insurance Escrows

It's common with residential properties for the lender to escrow taxes and insurance. For insurance, you'll pay the first year's premium in advance, plus an extra two months of premiums. Then, each month when you pay the loan payment, you also pay one month's insurance premiums. That way, when the premium is due in one year, there's enough money in the escrow account at the bank. Real estate taxes work in substantially the same way.

PMI Insurance

PMI stands for *private mortgage insurance*. If you don't have a 20% down payment, then you can still borrow money for a home purchase, but the lender will require PMI insurance. You pay the premium one time, at the beginning of the loan. If you default, and a foreclosure brings less than the full payoff on the loan, then the insurance company pays the difference between the 80% the bank would have loaned, and the 95% they actually loaned.

Taxes and Assessments

Assessments are bills to property owners for improvements—sewer, utilities, maybe a new swimming pool at a condominium. The seller might have paid some assessments in advance and might owe real estate taxes that are paid in arrears.

For items paid in advance by the seller, you'll have to reimburse him or her for that portion of the year you'll own the property. For items paid in arrears, like real estate taxes, you'll receive a credit for the bill you'll pay when it comes due. However, this really represents a portion of the year when the seller owned the property.

Title Insurance

The title insurance fee is based on the dollar amount of the insurance. Usually it's complicated to figure out, so you just have to call and ask for an estimate. If the title insurance company already wrote title insurance the *last* time that same property sold, then you can sometimes get what's called a *reissue credit*. In other words, you get a discount on the premium. When shopping for title insurance, ask if a company already has the title insured, and the amount of their reissue credit.

> ### Insight:
> Asking the right questions usually pays off. If your bank requires a certain title insurance company, but it's not the one that wrote the last policy, ask the title insurance company anyway: "Do you give a reissue credit even though you didn't write the old policy on this property?" Usually they'll say, "yes," as long as you provide them a copy of the old policy. If you don't ask, they won't volunteer the information and you don't get a credit.

Additional Fees

Origination fees are usually a percentage of the loan. These help the lender or originator cover the expenses associated with making a loan. *Discount fees* are also usually a percentage of the loan, and have to do with selling a loan on the secondary market. *Others fees* might be for an appraisal, inspection fee, survey, credit report, and termite bond, to name the most common ones.

Calculate Closing Costs

As discussed at the beginning of this chapter, obtain a copy of the HUD-1 and fill it out at the beginning of every property analysis. If the foreclosing bank is financing your purchase, then it should be willing to waive most of the fees and include the others in the loan amount. Foreclosing banks are pretty motivated to work something out with a credit-worthy borrower. There's no hard rule about who pays which expenses. It's all a matter of negotiation. If you don't know about the expenses in advance, though, you won't know to negotiate them.

Holding Costs of Investment Property

After the closing table, *holding cost* surprises account for the next biggest area of headaches. The money you have to pay until you can sell your property again is called your holding cost. Some items are obvious, like the interest you have to pay on the purchase money loan. Others are higher than expected, and some are downright hidden.

Insurance Expenses

The one that's overlooked most often is insurance. Insurance companies tend to think that vacant buildings are more likely to burn down than occupied buildings. Some companies won't even sell you insurance for a vacant building, at *any price*. Others make you pay through the nose for it.

You can alleviate the problem by making some repairs to the property, which qualifies you for contractor's insurance. Those premiums are usually fairly reasonable. The insurance company charges you, up front, for a one-year premium. If the property is completed before that time, you don't get a refund. Also, if the property is completed and you obtain a certificate of occupancy, the insurance cancels automatically as of that date.

On the other hand, you can at least obtain insurance at an affordable price. In all likelihood, you won't sell the property before the year's out anyway. Short-term investors typically hold their property for at least one year, so they can take advantage of capital gains tax rates. When you see an investor with properties in various stages of renovation that seem to be progressing pretty slowly, there's usually a good explanation. It has nothing to do with problems getting subcontractors to show up or with lack of funds until the investor's next regular paycheck arrives. It has to do with contractor's insurance, and with tax rates dependent on minimum holding periods.

Other Holding Costs

Other hidden holding costs might be utilities. Commercial customers usually pay higher utility rates than residential ones. Sometimes they also have to pay a minimum amount each month, no matter how small the usage. If you don't have a tenant in place to pay the utilities, you might find yourself stuck with high bills.

Other holding costs might include: lawn care, snow removal, pool maintenance, security, home owner's dues, real estate and school taxes, and any number of other governmental taxes. These continue with or without a tenant in place. If you have a house on the lake, you may have to pay a dock fee every year, whether you have a boat dock or not. Expenses such as trash pickup also must be paid whether you have trash or not. All of these types of expenses continue even if no one is living in the house. All are holding expenses for an investor.

Time Value of Money

Another hidden holding cost is the *time value* of your down payment. Suppose you pay could pay $25,000 down in order to purchase a property for $250,000 and resell it in a year for $275,000. Would you do it? In addition to calculating all your other expenses, for which you have to write checks, you also need to think about that $25,000 being tied up for one year. If it were in some investment earning 6% interest, it would earn $1,500 in one year. This has to be factored in as one of your holding expenses.

Remember that the goal of all this analysis is to avoid dangerous and costly surprises—and to give you the knowledge necessary to strike a fair deal with a borrower, instead of needing to steal property just in case dangerous and costly surprises rear their ugly heads.

The Fixer-Upper

It's not uncommon to find foreclosure properties with substantial deferred maintenance or repairs that have been let go for a long time. If someone doesn't have the money to make the mortgage payments, and probably suspects he or she is going to lose the property before too long, then routine repairs are not going to be made. This presents you with an opportunity and a problem.

The opportunity is that you can buy the property for some amount less than the fair market value, because of the deferred maintenance. A property's fair market value is determined based on its condition at the time of the proposed purchase *or* at the time of the appraisal. It's not uncommon to obtain an appraisal of what a property *will be* worth after a renovation, but those appraisals are clearly labeled as *postrenovation* appraisals.

Insight:

Most buyers do not have the imagination to look beyond cosmetic problems—paint, sheet rock damage, soiled carpets, and dated cabinet door styles—to see what a house could become, with very little time and money. The ones who have the imagination, don't have the time to do the work themselves, and don't have the confidence and knowledge to hire someone else. Because of this, easily fixable items can seriously depress the value of a house.

There are lots of books that tell you how to invest in fixer-uppers that you can find by searching the Internet. I don't want to duplicate that information. My goal in this chapter is to work through all the financial aspects of analyzing a fixer-upper property *before you buy it*, so you don't get hurt by any surprises.

One pleasant surprise has to do with financing. You can usually borrow 100% of the purchase price *and* the money for repairs if you're going to fix up a property. You have to do your homework and be able to demonstrate to the banker that the postrehab value of the property will result in an 80% loan-to-value—but that's usually fairly easy.

Repair Expenses

As far as estimating repair expenses, you cannot really rely on an *RFP—request for proposal*. Contractors can't give you a firm bids because they don't know what they'll run into in the process. If you insist on a firm bid, the contractor will add about 50% to 75% on top of what it *really* thinks it will take.

The best you can do is find honest and reputable repair people and then trust them, or do the work yourself. Typically, on any repair or renovation project, you'll need to estimate as best you can, and then add 10% to the overall budget for surprises. Don't plan on *saving* money when there are no surprises, because I've never known that to happen.

On page 168 is a worksheet to help you calculate how much it will cost to repair or renovate a property. It's organized in a way that architects and contractors use. That makes it look very professional if you need to show your budget to a banker in order to borrow money to do the work. If a banker doesn't know you, but all your paperwork looks neat, methodical, organized, and well-planned, then he or she will assume you are a neat, methodical, and organized person who meets commitments and doesn't get surprised.

Once you get beyond buying a personal residence, or a car, or obtaining a credit card, lending decisions don't rest exclusively on credit scores. They rely heavily on credibility, which can be demonstrated other ways than by a credit score.

Home improvement stores can help you come up with numbers for some of the items. You can also search the Internet and find websites with built-in calculators for estimating repairs. Do a search using *"home construction worksheet estimator."* This search will also bring up several software packages that will make the job easier.

If any item on this form doesn't apply to your project, just put a "0" in that block. Leave the item description on your form. It'll help as a type of checklist every time you use the form. Also, putting a "0" in a blank tells a banker you've thought about it and won't need to spend any money in that area. Otherwise, if he or she is familiar with this type of organization, he or she might just think you've forgotten about some expenses and underestimated the cost of the project.

Repair Calculation Worksheet

Item	Amount
General Requirements (Plans, insurance, engineering, building permits, temporary utilities, utility deposits, construction dumpster, final cleaning, small tools)	
Site Work (demolition, tree removal, paving, fences and gates, landscaping)	
Concrete (retaining walls, driveway repair)	
Masonry (bricks and repair, concrete blocks and repair, any equipment rental to do the work)	
Metals (metal fabrication, metal stairs, handrails and railings, ornamental metals)	
Rough Carpentry (wood framing, wood sheathing, wood decking)	
Finish Carpentry	
Millwork (trim, laminate countertops, work stations, cabinets, crown molding and ornamental woodwork)	
Thermal and Moisture Protection (waterproofing, vapor barriers, insulation, roofing)	
Doors and Windows	
Finishes (dry wall, tile or stone countertops, flooring, painting, wall coverings)	
Specialties (pest control, appliances, other miscellaneous stuff)	
Mechanical (plumbing, HVAC)	
Electrical (electrical service, light fixtures, phones, cable TV, security)	
Subtotal	
Allowance for over-runs (10%)	
Total Budget	

Finance the Cost

When doing your calculations for renovating a property, remember that you'll have no rental income while the repairs are being conducted. You'll still have all the holding costs of property ownership, though—insurance, utilities, and the rest. In addition, depending on how your loan is structured, you'll have interest payments to make every month.

One solution is to estimate how much your holding costs and interest expenses will be, and factor them into your loan request. This is very common in a development budget presented to a banker for a loan. Remember that banks are in the business of loaning the maximum amount of money they can justify based on the property value and your credit worthiness. If the numbers work out, they'd be *thrilled* to loan you enough money to pay all your expenses until a property sale or conversion to rental income.

An acquisition and renovation loan is typically structured with the first money being disbursed by the bank in order to buy the property. Then, you periodically (usually once every two weeks) submit bills to the bank for repairs up to that date. Make sure you cover with the banker, in advance, what their rules are for loan disbursements. You don't want to obtain financing from a lender that allows you to get money only once a month, or once every two weeks, but all your subcontractors expect to be paid weekly. You'll have to cover frequency of payment issues with both your bank, and your subcontractors, and get that nailed down before you make any commitments.

If the banks approves the bills, which they typically do, the bank will disburse enough money from the loan for you to pay the bills. Your chances of speedy approval can be improved significantly by taking the following steps.

- ◆ Use actual bills from your subcontractors, not a pretty list organized by you. Bills have credibility. A list could come from anywhere.
- ◆ Include a short statement regarding how much work remains to be done, how much it will cost you, and how long it will take.

The banker wants to know that you're staying within your budget and there haven't been any surprises.

♦ Include photographs of work progress. (Bankers love paper. The more paper you give them, the happier and more secure they feel.)

♦ Periodically ask if the banker would like to come out and inspect your property. Depending on the size of the project, he or she may take you up on it. They're supposed to do inspections on all renovation loans, but there's never enough time to go around for everything. (Simply making the offer gives you added credibility.)

Insight:

Construction lending is typically at higher interest rates than permanent financing, assuming both are adjustable rate loans. There may also be disbursal fees, inspection fees, and other hidden expenses. Be sure to ask up front, what all the fees for managing the loan will be, and budget accordingly.

Sales Cost

The expenses don't stop just because you have a buyer and the closing is scheduled for tomorrow. You will still have some deductions from your anticipated profit. They might include real estate sales commission, survey, appraisal, termite bond, mold/mildew bond, and shared closing expenses.

Most real estate contracts specify equal sharing of closing costs. Technically, closing costs are things like the closing attorney and document preparation, but some people might understand them to include all fees charged at a closing. *Loan costs* such as appraisal and survey should fairly belong to the buyer, as should recordation fees. Termite bonds and title insurance, which protect the buyer from disaster and protect the seller from being sued, are usually split equally. There are no hard and fast rules. Specify ahead of time who pays what.

The ultimate sales cost is the one that comes due on April 15th of every year. Remember to factor in tax consequences when calculating your profits on a resale of foreclosure property. You might qualify for long-term capital gains, short-term capital gains or, under some circumstances, you might be taxed at ordinary income rates. The rules are beyond the scope of this book, and they're subject to change. You can obtain them from IRS publications or on the IRS website at **www.irs.gov**.

Put the Pieces Together

You should think through the entire purchase-hold-sale process before you make any offers on foreclosure properties. The exercise will allow you to propose a realistic and fair, solution when feasible. People who can't analyze a property's true value and realistic expenses have no choice—they have to be bottom feeders in order to avoid unforeseen disasters. You're different. You can afford to be fair, because you'll be well-informed and confident. In addition, you'll be able to weed out rejects early and let borrowers go about their business of finding other solutions rather than placing false hope in your activities.

Here's a simplified worksheet incorporating most of the analytical tools you've gained so far.

Item	Amount
What can I sell the property for?	+ _____
What is the purchase price?	− _____
How much are the closing costs on purchase?	− _____
What are the holding expenses until I can sell?	− _____
What are the costs of repair/renovation?	− _____
Can I earn any rental income until sale?	+ _____
What are my expenses while I'm renting?	− _____
What are the closing costs on sale?	− _____
Grand Total:	= _____

Add or subtract each item, as the form requires. When you get to the bottom number, are you going to make money on the deal, and is it enough money to make it worth while?

If the answer is "yes," then ask yourself one final questions: Are you 95% certain that your numbers are accurate? If so, then you have a good investment. If the answer is "no," you should do more research in order to firm up your estimates, or possibly pass on the deal. Maybe 95% is more certainty than you require. If you've got a little bit of gambler in you, and can afford to exercise that instinct, then reduce your certainty ratio to something else, but increase the necessary profit margin slightly in order to provide a safety net.

Practice with these forms on some real transactions. If you know someone who's buying a house, ask him or her if you can estimate the closing expenses and then compare your worksheet to whatever it actually turns out to be. Look for some properties that are under contract, and see if you can figure out the fair market value. Compare your number to what those properties actually sell for. Repair and renovation expenses will be harder to practice, but you might have friends who will let you prepare your own estimates and then see how close you are to how the project turns out.

If you don't methodically work through all the worksheets, then you're just out there guessing about whether you'll make money or not. If you're guessing, then you need a really large margin of error and can't *afford* to be fair with property owners. Once you become comfortable that you can make a reasonable and consistent profit on your properties, then you can encourage partnerships with distressed property owners and let them share in those profits.

15

Structure a Deal with the Borrower

Now that you know what it's possible to do with a property, and have decided on your acquisition goals, it's time to strike a deal. There are three basic ways to do business with a borrower.

1. *No-Equity Asset Purchase*—Borrower has no equity and you persuade lenders to discount their debt.
2. *Equity Purchase*—Borrower has equity and you pay him or her something for his or her equity.
3. *Equity Repurchase*—Borrower has equity and you agree to let him or her buy the property back sometime in the future and recoup some of the equity.

California and Consumer Protections

Because of widespread abuses in the business of buying and selling distressed properties, many states are looking at legislative controls on the industry. Already, California has statutes in place to protect its citizens. I'll touch on those, briefly, even though they might not apply to you. You can expect more and more states to pass similar laws.

Under California law, a preforeclosure homeowner who agrees to sell his or her equity to someone else has a *grace period* to back out of the contract without penalty. The statute is lengthy and technical. If you want to read the whole thing, check out the California legislature's website at **www.leginfo.ca.gov** and look for Civil Code Section 1695.1695-17 (Home Equity Sales Contracts) and for 2945.2945-11 (Mortgage Foreclosure Consultants). Reprinted below is an excerpt from the first section. It will give you an idea of the low esteem in which the industry is held, thanks to the practices of certain individuals.

> *The Legislature finds and declares that homeowners whose residences are in foreclosure have been subjected to fraud, deception, and unfair dealing by home equity purchasers. The recent rapid escalation of home values, particularly in the urban areas, has resulted in a significant increase in home equities which are usually the greatest financial asset held by the homeowners of this state. During the time period between the commencement of foreclosure proceedings and the scheduled foreclosure sale date, homeowners in financial distress, especially the poor, elderly, and financially unsophisticated, are vulnerable to the importunities of equity purchasers who induce homeowners to sell their homes for a small fraction of their fair market values through the use of schemes which often involve oral and written misrepresentations, deceit, intimidation, and other unreasonable commercial practices.*

That's California, but the rest of the country can't be far behind. In Minnesota court cases have been filed and the legislature passed Minnesota General Statute 325N, regulating the buying and selling of foreclosure properties.

The fact that you may be subject to legislation should not be a cause of concern for you. All sorts of businesses are faced with regulations regarding their operation. However, you should be concerned with following the laws of your state. To find legislation in your state, call your state's Attorney General or State's Attorney and ask for the consumer affairs help desk. Tell them you're looking into buying foreclosure properties. Give them the citation to the California statute. Ask if there's anything similar in your state.

You'll also need to check pending legislation in order to see if something is working its way up through the process. Usually, your state legislative house will have some sort of consumer desk that can help you.

If you're comfortable doing Internet research, check out your state legislature. It probably has a website with a searchable database of statutes. Other times, lawfirms will post interesting consumer information on their websites. If your state doesn't have a searchable database of laws, then do a general Internet search. I've had good luck with *"foreclosure rescue services consumer protection."*

All of this research will help you learn about legislation, pending legislation, or trends in litigation.

Insight:

Trial attorneys share trade secrets with each other about potentially lucrative types of lawsuits. If some of them enjoy successes by suing foreclosure purchasers, then other lawyers will look for opportunities to do the same things. This doesn't mean you should avoid the whole concept, it just means you should learn from other people's mistakes. Plus, being ethical, fair, and compassionate isn't just morally proper—it's also good insurance!

The best way to avoid problems with a borrower is by full and fair disclosure followed by the borrower having a reasonable amount of private time to consult with loved ones and consider what you're offering. In order to avoid misunderstandings, and to show you're open and honest, use a plain language contract every time you decide to do business with a property owner. Written contracts provide the following benefits:

- they ensure everybody understands their rights and responsibilities;
- they force the parties to discuss all deal points;
- they supply legal recourse if someone backs out;
- they prove that everything was done in an ethical manner; and,
- they meet all safe harbor requirements, if available.

No-Equity Asset Purchase

This is the most common foreclosure scenario with homeowners. Borrowers are able to buy homes with little or nothing down, scrape by from month to month, and are then thrown into financial ruin with the slightest economic problem. There was never any equity and there isn't any now. Remember, too, that just because an owner made a sizeable down payment doesn't mean they *still* have equity. The property value might have declined in the meantime due to deferred maintenance or other factors.

If there's no equity, then the homeowner cannot reasonably expect to walk away with cash. You can offer other things, but not cash. Make sure you stress this often, in many different ways. You're not beating up the seller, you want him or her to understand he or she cannot walk away with cash. You'd be delighted if he or she could take home money, because it would mean the property's worth more than you thought. Be open to the seller's objections regarding value—he or she is prejudiced, certainly, but he or she might also be better informed than you.

In order to stress the no-equity status, you should mention it often. Here are some sample phrases you can use throughout the conversation:

- "Let me pull out my checklists for a no-equity transaction."
- "This is going to be a harder deal to accomplish because there's no equity."
- "In a typical no-equity situation, the bank is pretty motivated to work with people like me."

◆ "To some extent, not having any equity makes all your decisions simpler."

◆ "Just because you don't have any equity doesn't mean there's no hope."

◆ "Let's look at some ways to structure a no-equity deal."

Even with no equity, you *can* give the owner debt relief, dignity, bankruptcy avoidance, foreclosure avoidance, and preservation of some sort of credit score. Don't be bashful about pointing out these benefits. They are all extremely valuable and would cost the owner extra money in order to obtain. Use a worksheet similar to the one below to tally up some of the costs, so you can discuss the dollar value of what the borrower is getting.

$_____ If I can stop the interest clock from ticking away, right now, today, how much interest can I save you over the course of one month while we put this deal together?

$_____ If you filed for Chapter 13 in order to stop a foreclosure, you'd have to pay a lawyer a minimum of $500, plus the bankruptcy filing fees of $194.

$_____ Foreclosure will add at least another $1,500 in legal fees, notices, and related expenses. Even after foreclosure, you'll still have to pay these items or file for bankruptcy.

$_____ Once you have a foreclosure or bankruptcy on your credit file, some common expenses will increase. Insurance premiums and interest rates are tied to credit score. Utilities and landlords might require additional deposits. You'll be forced to use prepaid cell phones and secured credit cards.

These are just *hard dollar* items—things you can assign a definite value to. What's the value of avoiding public humiliation and embarrassment? How can you put a price tag on preserving some semblance of a good credit score, so you can finance a car or house in the future? If a borrower has no equity in the property, don't feel guilty about not paying them any money, because you're giving them other, equally valuable things.

Because you're a person who wants to do the right thing, don't get caught in the trap of doing too much. As an example, the house Jim is considering has an $85,000 mortgage payoff. In its present condition, it's worth around $83,000 to $85,000. There's no equity. If the borrower were current on his mortgage payments and sold the house, he wouldn't bring any cash home from the closing table. Jim's done his analysis and decided he can renovate the home after purchase and sell it for a profit. That analysis has nothing to do with the former owner. Jim is the one adding value to the property, not the borrower. Jim should not try to share the profits. That's going too far.

Suppose he's able to convince the lender to take only $70,000 to pay off the mortgage, and the lender agrees not to pursue the borrower for a $15,000 deficiency. Again, this has nothing to do with the borrower, who owned a no-equity property before Jim showed up and can't reasonably expect to make money just because Jim's now on the scene to do some sort of good deed. Jim, and you, shouldn't feel guilty about this—there's nothing unethical about it as long as you don't leave the borrower swinging in the wind on a deficiency!

If you bought a $70,000 house for $70,000, from someone not facing foreclosure, and then did a lot of painting, repairs, and landscaping, you would not feel guilty about selling it for $85,000 and keeping all the profits. Your personal efforts changed the financial picture regarding the house. It had nothing to do with taking advantage of the seller.

Write-Downs

When considering a *write-down* of the debt as a way to make the deal workable, be upfront with the seller. Say, "I will do this deal only if I can convince the lienholder to accept less than its full claim," or "I will do this deal only if I can buy the property for no more than the mortgage pay off *and* I can then improve it significantly and sell it at a profit." The seller should not care, because he or she is getting the benefit of the full value of the real estate. He or she is selling an $85,000 piece of property, and $85,000 in debt will go away.

Debt write-down carries some traps for the borrower. Caution the owner that this works only if he or she can show the IRS that he or she was insolvent before the write-down, and is still insolvent after the write-down. Debt-relief counts as income in the eyes of the IRS, unless you can fit through the loophole just described.

Insolvent is a funny word with a lot of different meanings. For purposes of the IRS loophole, your liabilities must exceed your assets in order to be insolvent. When doing the math, the only things that count as *assets* are things that hypothetical creditors might be able to seize.

NOTE: *If your retirement plan can't be attached by creditors in your state, then the plan doesn't count as an asset for determining if you are insolvent.*

To be even more complicated, you can be a little bit insolvent. The IRS *safe harbor* for debt relief income shelters the seller against debt relief taxable income *only* to the extent of the insolvency. The following example will help you understand the limits on the safe harbor.

Remember that Jim is considering buying a preforeclosure house with $85,000 due in order to payoff the mortgage. The borrower has $85,000 in mortgage debt and he also has credit card debt of $20,000. His only asset is the house.

Total assets:	+$85,000
Total liabilities:	−$105,000
Net worth	−$20,000

The borrower is insolvent by $20,000. (He might be described as *$20,000 under water* or *$20,000 in the red*.)

If Jim is successful in getting the bank to write down the sellers debt to $70,000, and not seek a deficiency, that's $15,000 worth of debt relief for the borrower. The borrower is *under water* or insolvent by $20,000, but he has only $15,000 of debt relief, so he fits into the safe harbor and has no taxable income. In other words, making $15,000 worth of debt disappear doesn't miraculously cure the borrower of being insolvent.

On the other hand, $25,000 of debt relief would be $5,000 *more* than his insolvency. If $25,000 worth of debt went away, this is what the borrower's financial position would look like:

Total assets:	+85,000
Liabilities after write-down:	−80,000
Net worth	$5,000

The borrower would be solvent by $5,000 (on paper), so he has to pay taxes on $5,000 worth of income, even though he never received any cash. To learn more, read IRS Publication 908, which you can find online at **www.irs.gov**.

You need to understand these concepts so you can work together with the seller. Tell the seller that debt relief normally counts as income. Give him or her a copy of IRS publication 908. Say there is a loophole, but you need to pave the way in advance in order to take advantage of it.

In the $15,000 write-down example, the lienholder will send a 1099-C form to the homeowner and to the IRS showing $15,000 in debt relief income. If the seller/taxpayer can't fit into the safe harbor, he or she will have to report this as income on Form 1040. If he or she qualifies for the safe harbor, there's not a separate form to explain it, the taxpayer simply doesn't report the item as income.

If the seller thinks he or she will qualify for the loophole, he or she should do a worksheet of assets and liabilities immediately before and after the sale, and keep it in a safe place for when he or she prepare his or her tax returns, along with copies of any documents showing values of assets and amounts of liabilities.

You should warn the borrower that there are lots of people promoting complicated schemes for *tricking* the IRS, getting debt relief, and making life wonderful again. Usually, the property owner has to pay a fee, upfront, to take advantage of those programs. Explain that these things are largely scams. If something looks too good to be true, it's not true. You're offering something real, legal, tax-free, and valuable—but you both have to do your homework.

Sign a Deal

The following is a list of points that must be discussed and agreed upon in a no-equity deal:

- ❏ the value of the property before any discussions about how to structure a deal;
- ❏ a disclosure of the tax consequences of debt relief and the seller's responsibility to satisfy him- or herself that he or she can fit within the safe harbor;
- ❏ permission to run a credit report and lien search to determine all creditors, spouse, etc.;
- ❏ a waiver of financial privacy laws and permission for you to speak with lenders;
- ❏ a recognition that the owner should obtain his or her own independent legal and accounting advice because you are not his or her agent, representative, or partner;
- ❏ a timetable for reaching a written agreement with all lien-holders;

❑ the consequences of not reaching a deal with lienholders by a *drop dead date*—you may proceed with your efforts, but the property owner should pursue other alternatives and will no longer be obligated to do business with you;

❑ an agreement that your contract continues until there's a foreclosure or bankruptcy;

❑ if you're in a postforeclosure right of redemption state, an agreement that the owner will assign his or her right of redemption to you if there is a foreclosure, and the amount you will pay for that right;

❑ possession of the property—what happens to the owner after purchase; and,

❑ anything else that seems pertinent to the situation.

Insight:

There's nothing complicated or magic about writing contracts. List any important questions you asked the other party and the answers they gave you. Call this section "Representations." Next, write down everything you agreed to do; everything they agreed to do; and, the time limits for doing things. Call this section "Agreements." Finally write down what happens if someone doesn't do what they're supposed to do. Call this section "Default." Sign at the end, and you have a contract.

Make *sure* you stress to the seller that you'll do your best, but sometimes these things don't work out. Remember, you're dealing with someone who's in a very tough situation. They'd like to believe that you will save them, but you might not. They need to understand they should continue to explore other alternatives, up to and including bankruptcy or foreclosure.

If you don't have agreements with lienholders by the drop dead date, give your Referrals Letter to the property owner.

Equity Purchase

As in a no-equity situation, the first step is to reach an agreement about what the property's worth. If there are $100,000 in liens, you think the property's worth $125,000, but the owner thinks it's worth $200,000, then you're probably not going to be able to reach any agreement regarding the value of their equity. If there is equity in the property you may be able to enter into an *equity purchase.*

If you decide to go forward with an equity purchase, bear in mind that you can pay the agreed amount at closing, in payments over time, or when you re-sell the property. Following are some different reasons sellers might prefer one method over another. You'll have to educate them about the pros and cons of each situation, and why you think the one you're proposing would be best for everyone.

Cash Now

Cash-in-hand *always* seems like the best answer if you are the seller. However, if the seller has other creditors (ex-spouses, IRS, etc.) who learn that a large amount of money is coming in the future, the creditors can always send a garnishment to you and grab all of it. For you, the buyer, cash now is usually better because it makes a clean break with the seller. You have no further obligations and no further opportunity for something to go wrong.

Payments Over Time

A seller might prefer payments because it gives him or her a regular income to count on until he or she can get back on his or her feet or make other arrangements. Depending on the amount, the payments might be exempt from garnishment. Generally, the payments would be small enough to pass under the radar of most creditors.

In addition, even after your transaction, the seller might still need to file Chapter 13 for various reasons. To do so he or she has to have a regular income to qualify. Your payments may be the regular income that will allow him or her to qualify for Chapter 13 protection and keep his or her car and other property, for example.

You, as the buyer might like this approach because it allows you to buy the property, rent it out, and pay the seller out of the rental income. Even if you rent the property back to the former owner, you can write your payment check each month to the former owner, and have him endorse it back to you as a credit on the rent.

Payment in the Future

Sometimes, you simply can't afford to pay the seller any money until you're able to sell the property in the future. If that's the case, tell the seller. Don't try to convince the seller that it is the best deal for him or her, or that you are a tough operator and it's the *only* way you'll do a deal. You are helping him or her and should not be embarrassed by the manner in which you can provide that help.

Even if you can afford to pay the seller now, you might be afraid to because the property might not be worth what you think. Be honest about that, also.

When structuring a deal in which you pay the owner for his or her equity, evaluate the minimum amount you'd have to make in order for all your work to be worth doing. Don't settle for just that amount, but if the seller wants too much, then you need to move on. Use thee value of Equity Worksheet on the following page to help evaluate how much to offer the seller for his or her equity.

Value of Equity Worksheet

Agreed value of seller's equity   + _____

Expenses associated with stopping the foreclosure
(correspondence, long distance calls, travel & auto, etc.)   – _____

A modest and reasonable dollar value for your time in
stopping the foreclosure, because otherwise you could
spend your time working on some other deal   – _____

Expenses associated with any new loan(s) to replace the
Seller's mortgage(s), if that proves necessary   – _____

Cleanup and repairs to make the property marketable,
(but do not include here the cost of improvements to
make the property more valuable)   – _____

Holding costs until you can reasonably expect to sell
the property (this figure would be "0" if you are buying
the property for yourself and have no plans to sell)   – _____

Costs of sale, including closing expenses and real estate
commissions (this figure would be "0" if you are buying
the property for yourself and have no plans to sell)   – _____

The minimum amount you have to make in order for
you to spend time and money doing this deal   – _____

What's left over to divide   = _____

Don't show this form to the seller unless he or she rejects what you consider a fair offer. If the seller is predisposed to accept your offer, then revealing your calculations might cause misunderstandings and a desire for more money. Rejection, on the other hand, calls for reinforcements. You might want to share your form, and its numbers, in order demonstrate that your offer is reasonable.

As with the no equity transaction, you should have a checklist of items to cover, and you should incorporate them into a contract. The following is a checklist that you should be able to turn into a contract.

- ❑ The value of the property before any discussions about how to structure a deal
- ❑ How much the seller will be paid for his or her equity, and when/how that money will be paid
- ❑ Permission to run a credit report and lien search to determine all creditors, spouse, etc.
- ❑ A waiver of financial privacy laws and permission for you to speak with lenders in order to obtain accurate payoff information and/or the possibility of assuming the loans
- ❑ A recognition that the owner should obtain his or her own independent legal and accounting advice because you are not his or her agent, representative, or partner
- ❑ A timetable for a due diligence period, during which you can cancel the contract at any time without consequences if you discover something that makes it unworkable, but after which you're fully obligated to buy
- ❑ A time table for closing after completion of the due diligence, and consequences of not closing on time
- ❑ Possession after purchase
- ❑ Anything else that seems pertinent to the situation, including any state disclosures

Equity Repurchase

In an *equity repurchase*, you give the borrower the opportunity to buy the property back from you. First, a word of warning. There are thousands of scams that promise to let a distressed seller buy the property back in the future. They generally include huge markups on the purchase price, hidden expenses that have to be reimbursed, and back doors that let the foreclosure buyer wiggle out if the former owner makes one misstep in the process.

You don't need to resort to that. As a practical matter, the seller has little probability of being able to buy the property back. Sure, he or she has high hopes and lots of optimism, but it just doesn't usually work out that way. A superficially ethical person would rest on that, let the former owner think he or she can buy the property back, and then sit back confident it's not going to happen. A truly ethical person will warn the seller that it rarely works out; ask him or her to take a day or two and really think about the realistic likelihood of being able to come up with the money in the time required; and, if the seller remains confident, then go forward with your negotiations.

To move forward you first need to calculate the purchase price and the time limit for exercising the right to buy the property back. The reason you have to agree on a time limit is because you now have money tied up in this property that you could be using to make money some place else. The longer it is in this property, you are losing other opportunities you could have with this money.

The time limit should be expressed in a manner similar to the following: "Closing on the repurchase must take place on or before four o'clock p.m., Central Time, on March 13, 2006." The reason you're this specific is you don't want any mistakes. Suppose you say that repurchase has to happen within four months. This is September 12th. Does that mean by January 11th, January 12th, January 13th, or January 31st? Any one of them could be right, depending on the circumstances and what's typical in your community.

A worksheet for evaluating the transaction follows on the next page.

Equity Repurchase Worksheet

Your purchase price (usually, the payoff on the mortgages
and other liens)   + _____

Expenses associated with stopping the foreclosure
(correspondence, long distance calls, travel & auto, etc.)   + _____

Expenses associated with any new loan(s) to replace
the Seller's mortgage(s), if that proves necessary   + _____

Expenses associated with purchasing from the seller,
including all closing costs and title insurance   + _____

Cleanup and repairs to make the property rentable if you
are going to rent it out until the seller buys it back from you   + _____

Expenses to make the property more valuable, but only
if you both agree that this should be done in order to attract
renters in the meantime   + _____

Holding costs until end of the time period during
which the seller can rebuy from you   + _____

Costs of sale back to the original owner, including
all closing costs and title insurance   + _____

The minimum amount you have to make in order
for you to spend time and money doing this deal   + _____

The *lowest* number you'll have to get in order
to sell the property back to the original owner   = _____

After you do your analysis, you and the seller should agree on the following items and incorporate them into a contract.

- ❏ The value of the property before any discussions about how to structure a deal
- ❏ The repurchase price, time limit, and terms, such as all cash in certified funds, or some combination of certified funds and you holding a mortgage
- ❏ Whether the seller will continue to occupy the property, and the terms of the lease
- ❏ Permission to run a credit report and lien search to determine all creditors, spouse, etc.
- ❏ A waiver of financial privacy laws and permission for you to speak with lenders in order to obtain accurate payoff information and/or the possibility of assuming the loans
- ❏ A recognition that the owner should obtain his own independent legal and accounting advice because you are not his agent, representative or partner
- ❏ A timetable for a due diligence period, during which you can cancel the contract at any time without consequences if you discover something that makes it unworkable, but after which you're fully obligated to buy
- ❏ A time table for closing after completion of the due diligence, and consequences of not closing on time
- ❏ Anything else that seems pertinent to the situation, including state disclosures

16

Structure a Deal with the Lender

Your negotiations don't end with the owner—you also have to strike deals with lenders. Maybe all you want is to borrow money to fund your purchase. Perhaps you must convince the mortgage holder to accept less than a full payoff. Either way, you have to understand lenders and know what they need to make them happy.

Lenders are uncomplicated creatures. With them, if the numbers work, they'll do it. If the numbers don't work, they won't do it. Your job is to convince a lender that your numbers are realistic.

Lenders want three things:

1. to maximize assets and income;
2. to minimize risk and expenses; and,
3. to protect themselves if they don't meet one and two.

Insight:

I'll let you in on a secret about lenders. It's easier to borrow millions of dollars to buy a shopping center or office building than it is to borrow $200,000 for a fourplex. The larger the loan, the more likely the evaluation will be based strictly on net operating income, and not the borrower's credit score or income. (Don't think too small when looking for investments. Don't be afraid of banks.)

Maximize Assets and Income

A loan is an *asset* to a bank. A loan that goes bad is an asset that's going away. Just getting the cash back isn't a complete answer for the bank, because then they have to find another customer to whom they can loan money. Think about it—spare cash is a problem for banks. They have to send their cash out to work, to earn an income.

What does this mean to you? Banks are motivated to obtain as many assets as possible, and therefore, they are motivated to finance *you* when you buy a foreclosure property. For a lender, financing your acquisition is a case of turning lemons into lemonade. Not only do they get their money back on a bad loan, but they can also charge new fees and book another asset. Always approach the original lender first about financing a foreclosure purchase.

Minimize Risk and Expenses

Some lenders, such as the large pools on the secondary market, are not set up to handle individual mortgages. They don't have the personnel, the lawyers, or the systems and procedures. Their primary motivation is to minimize risk and expenses. They expect a certain number of loans to go bad. It's part of the cost of doing business. The trick is to cut their losses as soon as possible and move on. If a workout looks efficient (easy), they'll do it. If not, they'll foreclose and sell the deficiency to a collection agency. With any lender, the longer they *fool with* a bad loan, the more likely it will cost them money, someone will sue, or the manager will be criticized by his superiors.

What does this mean to you? You can help a lender minimize risk and expenses by doing this work for him or her. If you supply every conceivable piece of information about a property, your plans for it, and all the details regarding what you want from the lender, then you have a very high likelihood of success. Remember, too, that neatness counts.

The process I'm going to describe is called "papering the file." Lenders are comforted by fat files, auditors are delirious with joy, and file room clerks rest easy with the confidence of perpetual job security.

Insight:

The more paper you can generate to fill files, the more you will be helping peace and goodwill on earth.

Start by putting every presentation to a banker into a three-ring binder. Some people like to use a more permanent type of binding, but not me. The goal, you'll remember, is to make it easy on the lender. He or she can't copy individual pages easily with a difficult binder. Also, have preprinted index dividers with numbered tabs corresponding to a table of contents.

The binder itself must have a pocket on the inside of the cover, so you can put a CD in there. Burn onto the CD all spreadsheets used in your presentation and all photo files. Most of the time, bankers must insert data into their own forms. It's easier if they can import it from your file, instead of having to rekey everything. The lender can email your photos to appraisers, if necessary, thereby speeding up that part of the process.

At a minimum, the following information should go into every package you give a lender.

- ❏ Cover letter setting out your request
- ❏ Information about you and any relevant experience
- ❏ Your personal financial statement—assets and liabilities
- ❏ Property legal description and street address
- ❏ Photographs of the property
- ❏ Evaluation of comparable sales and/or NOI
- ❏ Your plans for the property
- ❏ How you'll fund the mortgage payments each month

If your goal is to borrow money, then provide the last several years' tax returns. Include a section with cash flow analysis if you're buying income-producing property. Information about any tenants is important. For properties you intend to improve, devote a section of the binder to your "Capital Budget," or the money you intend to spend on the site, and another section for the post-improvement value. Those of you trying to persuade a mortgage holder to accept less money—called a *write-down*—will need to include some information about why the property is worth less than the debt. In addition, you want to convince the lender that the borrower is totally insolvent and not worthy of pursuit for a deficiency.

> **Insight:**
> If you sell yourself as a solution to the lender's problem, he or she will generally let you be the solution.

For a write-down *and* a loan, prepare two different three-ring binders. The banker might need to obtain different approvals for the two tasks. You never know, it might be easier for him or her to secure all the necessary authorizations if the left hand, so to speak, doesn't know what the right hand is doing.

Protect Themselves

All of these things assist the banker in his or her final motivator of protecting him- or herself if something goes wrong. Face it, the lender does not have time to personally check out everything—and anything that can't be confirmed is something that could blow up in his or her face in the future. The more information you give a lender, the more comfortable he or she becomes that there won't be any surprises on down the road. In addition, if others in the lender's office have also reviewed the package, and agreed that everything possible is in it, then future criticisms from a boss can be met with, *Well, you looked at the same thing I reviewed, and you didn't see any problems.*

> **Insight:**
> Having a solution is a larger motivational tool *before* the foreclosure notice goes out than afterwards. If you can work with a lender to reach a solution *before* the loan has to be written down, then you have a better likelihood of working out a deal.

17

Go to Foreclosure Sales

When foreclosure seems inevitable, you can sometimes buy properties fairly cheaply at the foreclosure auction, especially if you're well prepared. Whether you buy before, during, or after the auction, you pretty much need to do the same things to be prepared.

On the day of the foreclosure, a representative of the lender will stand on the courthouse steps and announce that they are proceeding. Most of the time, the representative will be the only person present. Sometimes there's a small group of interested bidders, or even just *tourists*—those just there to watch. The lender's representative will then usually read the foreclosure ad and ask for bids. He or she may start with the bank's bid, or there might be a second representative from the bank, to make the bid. Even if no one else is there, he or she will look around expectantly, ask if there are any other bids, wait a few seconds, and then announce that the bank is the high bid. Then everyone goes back to the office.

Practice First

I recommend calling to get information on a few foreclosures *before* you find something that *really* interests you as a possible purchase. You'll get a little practice gathering information and talking to the attorneys or trustees. That way, when it's important, you won't sound like some hick who just fell off the turnip truck. You'll be smooth, polished, and matter-of-fact when you smoothly ask, "Is this lender interested in receiving my RFP (request for proposal) in order to bid on the financing terms for a potential acquisition of the foreclosed property?" Compare that with, "Um, I was kinda wondering if the bank would loan the money for me to buy the property?" Which person would *you* rather do business with?

Go to Sales

Even if you aren't yet ready to buy any particular property, start going to local foreclosure sales. You'll get a sense of the players involved, the local etiquette regarding how things are done, and what happens when it rains. Bad weather usually has an effect on how many bidders show up and how much time the attorney takes trying to jack the price up among competing bidders. This is all good information to know before it becomes real for you with your own purchase.

Don't be bashful when you start going to foreclosure auctions. Walk around and meet the other bidders before the sale. Obtain names and business cards, if available. Pay attention to what the other bidders do, and who the players are. You might find a terrific opportunity later that's too large to handle by yourself. If you know the names of other people who attend foreclosure auctions, you might be able to strike up a partnership.

Foreclosure auctions, like all auctions, are tricky situations. You could get something valuable for pennies on the dollar, or you could buy a lemon. Do your homework, and then establish a *preferred price* and an *upper limit price*. If your preferred price is $85,000 but the bidding exceeds that, take a few moments to evaluate. Don't be bashful—ask the auctioneer if you can have two minutes to collect your thoughts. He or she might actually give it to you. If you're ambivalent about the property—you could take it or leave it—then stop when the preferred price is reached. If you really want it, then continue bidding until you reach your predetermined upper limit.

Even if another bidder exceeds your upper limit by only $100, STOP bidding. Sure, the other bidder might buy the property for only $100 more than you were willing to spend, but you can't kick yourself. The other bidder might have continued escalating the price until he or she finally won, or until you finally found yourself the successful bidder at a price you couldn't realistically afford.

The Anxious Lender

The last thing before the actual foreclosure is a round of public notices in a newspaper or at the courthouse. If anything happens to delay a foreclosure, then the whole cycle of notices has to start all over. That's generally at least a three-week delay.

Insight:

I've seen foreclosures carried out in the driving rain only hours before a full blown hurricane was due to hit! Wind, hail, tornado warnings—they mean nothing to a bank in a hurry. That's good for you, though, because very few buyers turn out in bad weather. You and the auctioneer might be all alone, and the price might be right.

Lenders get in a hurry for a variety of reasons. Once you understand why, you won't spend so much energy trying to figure out hidden agendas, such as whether or not the bank's trying to unload the property before someone discovers toxic waste on it.

The number one reason lenders want to hurry a foreclosure along is because the loan officer's performance review is based on the age of his or her nonperforming assets. (It's a mouthful, but that's how bankers talk. In lending, an *asset* is a loan.) When the statistics are tallied up for year-end bonuses, a banker doesn't get to explain that his or her foreclosures took longer than anyone else's because his or her courthouse got blown away in a tornado and he or she didn't have any courthouse steps on which to conduct an auction. To the bank, the average age of the banker's nonperforming assets was longer than anyone else's, so no bonus.

Rushing to be First

Sometimes a lender is in a hurry because it's trying to beat the clock before someone else files another lien. Usually, the first to file a lien beats out everyone afterwards, but there are exceptions. Under some circumstances, a contractor or repair person can file what's called a *mechanics' and materialmen's lien* and it's superior to a first mortgage. That person can foreclose and wipe out the bank's loan.

If the IRS files a lien, then everything has to stop while the bank gives the IRS extra notice of the foreclosure. The IRS doesn't come first, but it can sure cause some long delays. Divorce can stop a foreclosure if one of the divorcing parties asks the court to issue an order halting the auction until further notice.

Finally, there's the ever-present risk of bankruptcy. Of course, a borrower can file *after* the foreclosure and have it set aside, but that's rare. Once the auction takes place, people generally give up.

After the Auction

When the auction is over, the winning bidder pays cash for the full purchase price, unless prior arrangements have been made. Those prior arrangements must be in writing. That's not a legal requirement, but a smart person requirement. Sometimes buyers hear what they want to hear, and sometimes sellers like to give the impression they've said more than they really did. A letter or memo takes out all of the wiggle room for misinterpretations.

Most normal real estate sales contracts have something called a *financing contingency*. A written clause says, if you can't borrow money to complete the purchase, you can cancel the contract and get your earnest money back. Foreclosure auctions are like any other auction—no contract, no negotiations, no time to get your money together. A purchaser who cannot make good on his or her bid, and buy the property, can be sued. The lender will ask for damages equal to all the expenses of a new foreclosure, and interest on your bid price. It will also ask for the difference between your bid price and the actual selling price, in the event the property brings less than your bid at the next auction.

The lesson here is, find out in advance what the payment arrangements are. If you don't have the money already lined up and locked in, don't play in that game. Wait for another auction.

The Deed

Assuming there are no problems and you proceed to closing, you'll receive a special type of deed. A normal, everyday deed has *covenants* or promises that say no one else has any claim or interest in the property. The lender doesn't want to make those promises, because it doesn't really know. The foreclosure deed will simply promise that the *lender* is not making any more claims to the property. Anything else, you take at your own risk. This doesn't need to be a scary thing for you, you just need to know about it so you can take steps to protect yourself. Chapter 11 contains this information.

Redemption Rights

The foreclosure process doesn't always end when the gavel comes down at auction. Some states give their residents a right to buy properties back, even after a foreclosure. You should be aware that the phrase "right of redemption" means different things in different states. In some states, it mean that the defaulting borrower has a right to "redeem him- or herself" and get current on the loan before the gavel drops at a foreclosure. Other states use the expression to mean the repurchase option after a foreclosure. To find out what the law is in your state, consult a title company, a mortgage lender, or other real estate professionals.

If postforeclosure redemption is available, it means that a former owner can force you to sell the property back to them, within a certain amount of time, by paying your bid price plus interest at a predetermined legal rate. Usually, the interest rate is much higher than market rates at the time.

Sometimes, other lienholders can also redeem the property. Let's say you go to auction and buy a $100,000 house for $40,000. The owner moved to Barbados, so you're not worried about him or her. But, the house also had a $20,000 second mortgage, wiped out in the auction. In other words, the second lender received nothing, because there wasn't enough money to go around after the first mortgage was paid from your purchase funds. The junior lienholder—or second mortgagee—might find someone who's willing to pay $65,000 for that same house. So, the lienholder will redeem the property from you for $40,000 plus interest, sell it to someone else for $65,000, and be able to recover the amount of its loan out of the $25,000 surplus. If you live in a state that allows this, it depresses the foreclosure prices because of the uncertainty whether a bidder will be able to keep the property or not.

If you're an investor, a right of redemption after foreclosure isn't necessarily bad. It means that, if the bank has to bid in the property, they're probably not going to be able to sell it until after the redemptory period expires. That can be as long as a year. Very few people want to buy a house, for example, if they might have to move out in a year or less. The situation softens the lender up a lot, so they're more motivated to work with you and get you to buy the property before or during the auction.

It also means that you don't necessarily have to buy properties at auction. If something looks like a terrific deal, but there's not enough time to analyze it, you might want to buy the former owner's right of redemption. Someone else, or even the bank, can buy the property at the auction. At any time during the redemptory period, you can pay the former owner several thousand dollars, or offer to split profits with him or her, and buy his or her right of redemption.

Suppose a bank has a foreclosure auction on a $125,000 house. The successful bidder is a third party, who pays $95,000. You want the house. In a postforeclosure redemption state, you can pay the former owner $1,000 (or whatever it takes) and buy his or her redemptory rights. That entitles you to pay the successful bidder $95,000, plus a few months of interest on that sum, and force him or her to sell the property to you.

I don't recommend it in the case of a third party buyer, because it's a pretty slick practice, and feels slightly unethical, to force a good faith buyer to sell you his or her property. You might comfort yourself with the thought that the third party buyer receives his or her principal and interest, but if there were other costs, such as closing and loan expenses, then that money is gone forever. The third party buyer doesn't get reimbursed for those expenses.

If the lender bid the property in at auction, and then wants a high price to sell it to you, that changes the equation. I don't think it's fair for a bank to profit on foreclosure real estate. It would be a different matter if they gave the borrower a credit for the profit the lender makes when it resells property after auction, but it doesn't work that way. The bank makes a profit, and it still pursues the borrower for a deficiency. I have no problem buying a post-foreclosure right of redemption so I could then buy the property directly from the bank.

When Not to Buy

There's a loophole I'll explain later, but two types of people should never buy property at a foreclosure auction in a state with post-foreclosure rights of redemption. People who want to buy a house to live in should not buy unless they're okay with the risk that they might have to find something else if the borrower redeems. (Statistically, it's rare, but it does happen.) The other off-limits auction buyer is someone who needs to flip properties—buy and sell them pretty quickly—in order to survive. Usually, such people borrow 100% of the purchase money on a six-month loan, with all the principal and interest due at the end of the period. They depend on selling the real estate in order to get the money to pay back the loan. If they can't sell because people are scared off by the redemption rights, then they'll have to go back to the bank and ask for an extension or renewal of the note. They don't always get it.

The loophole comes from the fact that, under some circumstances, the former owner can lose his or her right of redemption. First, the former owner might have lost his or her rights of redemption through failure to comply with some technicalities in the law. For example, in some states the new owner can send a certified letter to the old owner and give him or her ten days to vacate the property. If he or she doesn't, then the former owner loses his or her right of redemption. Keep this in mind when buying redemptory rights from borrowers—they might not exist any more. You might be buying nothing. Second, other people might have rights of redemption that can be purchased, and the new purchasers might be able to force you to sell! If you're relatively new to foreclosure purchases, I recommend staying away from buying rights of redemption. You'll probably get hurt, or end up hurting someone else.

Possible Changes

You should be aware of some changes coming in the law. The National Conference of Commissioners on Uniform State Laws is an organization that examines legal problems on a national scale and then recommends legislation that can be passed by individual states in order to avoid those problems. Model legislation includes the *Uniform Residential Mortgage Foreclosure Act* and the *Uniform Nonjudicial Foreclosure Act*.

The Uniform Laws Commissioners believe that traditional foreclosures are one-sided and oppressive. They would like to see a mechanism by which foreclosure sale prices can be negotiated, or at least bring bids in line with appraisals that have built-in safeguards for the borrower. They also recommend that lenders be required to make greater disclosures to buyers about title research and preforeclosure appraisals. Both of those things should reduce uncertainty and increase bid prices.

You might want to track your own state legislation to see if these proposed laws are under discussion. Your representative in the state legislature should be able to assist you with information. In addition, most state law-making bodies have their own website, on which you can search for laws currently in committee, or coming up for a vote.

Deficiencies

With traditional foreclosures, or the up-and-coming negotiated foreclosures, losing their property is not the end of the bad news. Remember, from earlier, that the bank gives the borrower a credit against his or her loan for the bid price of the property. If that's not enough to pay off the loan, then the left over amount is called a deficiency. Most times, a lender can sue for the deficiency and seize other property or garnish wages. *Some* state laws forbid deficiencies when a home is foreclosed. Proposed federal legislation would abolish such protections, in all states, when a federal loan is foreclosed.

A lender might not sue *immediately* to recover a deficiency. A promissory note is a contract, so a lawsuit for a deficiency is a lawsuit on a contract. Most states have very long statutes of limitations for contract suits, and very short ones for torts such as fraud and negligence. A smart bank will wait until the statute of limitations has expired for all torts, and then file suit "in contract" for the deficiency. That way, the borrower doesn't have any claims it can assert against the lender in order to create bargaining leverage. You must make the borrower realize that because he or she doesn't have anything to lose *today* if there's a deficiency, doesn't mean that will always be the case.

18

Buy after Foreclosure

Finding properties *before* foreclosure will usually offer the best opportunities, but it takes a hefty time commitment on your part. Sometimes you just can't afford that, and are willing to accept a smaller profit on your investments or pay a somewhat higher price for a home. You can still buy properties *after* the foreclosure sale. As an additional benefit, there's no more heartache or emotional turmoil involved in the acquisition. The former owner's lost the property, moved out, and you're just shopping, pure and simple. But the question remains, *Where do you shop?*

Local Lenders' ORE Departments

Call around to the banks and credit unions in town to find out who's in charge of their foreclosed real estate, usually in the Owned Real Estate or ORE department. Ask if there's anything in inventory right now, or if they're expecting anything in the near future. Sometimes lenders won't talk to you, but will refer you to a real estate agent in town who handles all their OREs. That's okay, just call the agent. Other times a banker will try to sell property directly to you and save the agent's commission. You should get a sense of who does what, so you know where to concentrate your efforts.

Property Magazine

In the Showcase of Homes or similar property listing magazine, there is not a section called "Foreclosed Properties." You'll have to look at all the pictures and read all the descriptions in order to discover the ones you want. This isn't all bad, because it's part of your education process regarding average selling prices. Sometimes the ad will have the word "Foreclosure" stamped across the top, sometimes it will be in the body. Almost always the ad mentions foreclosure somewhere.

> **Insight:**
> Just because a real estate ad says "foreclosure," doesn't mean it's being offered at a bargain basement price. The reason real estate agents include the word "foreclosure" is to *create the impression* that it's a discounted property.

Following Up on Foreclosure Notices

Keep track of the foreclosure notices in your paper or at the courthouse. Contact the lenders or their attorney and ask to be notified if the bank bids on the property and has it available for sale. Be sure to call again a day or so after the foreclosure was scheduled. You can also check the real estate records to see if a foreclosure deed has been recorded. Remember, we live in an age of information overload, too much work, not enough hours in the day, and the resulting very high likelihood that someone might have misplaced your name and telephone number. Don't be discouraged by a failure to return calls, just be persistent.

Government Foreclosures

Bear in mind you can call all the government agencies and ask to be put on their foreclosure sale mailing lists. It's not a very efficient way to shop, but it might be all that's possible for you. To research government foreclosures on the Internet, go to **www.hud.gov/homes/homesforsale.cfm**. This is a Web page for the Department of Housing and Urban Development. They also have links to foreclosure sale pages for VA, FDIC, GSA, IRS, SBA, US Army Corps of Engineers, US Customs, US Marshall's Service, the Department of Agriculture Rural Development, and something called "related links" to Fannie Mae and Freddie Mac. These are all agencies that either make mortgage loans, insure loans, or foreclose on liens, like the IRS.

Property Search at Courthouse

The major bank in my part of the country is AmSouth. If I wanted to know what foreclosed real estate AmSouth owned, I would go to the courthouse (or online, if courthouse records are searchable that way) and do a search of all real estate owned by AmSouth in my county. Some of it will be branch banks, but the rest will be foreclosed real estate. You might want to try this route if you can't get anyone to return your phone calls.

19

What Happens after the Purchase

Many times an owner is so focused on the trauma of the impending foreclosure that he or she has not really made any plans for life after the sale. It's vitally important to you, because you need to make plans for making your mortgage payments on time, fixing up the property, moving in yourself, and/or selling it.

You should have noticed by now a consistent theme throughout this book of people working together to solve problems and reach goals. In order to successfully negotiate a mutually satisfying arrangement, you *must* understand the other person's goals. Many times he or she will not able to articulate them well, or perhaps not even thought about them. You can help, especially as it relates to the possession issue.

Ask questions about postpurchase plans. Sometimes you need to look behind the words, and ask searching questions, in order to discover the *true* goals or the hidden agendas. What follows are some problems former owners might voice and some suggestions for solutions.

I won't have anyplace else to live.

From your analysis of property values, you may have discovered comparable properties available for rent. At the very least, keep a list of contacts you can call in order to find rental homes or apartments for a departing owner.

Section 8 housing might be a possibility. Be part of the solution, not part of the problem.

I can't afford a security deposit someplace else.

Point out that he or she would need a security deposit to rent from you. Unless it's a no-equity situation, offer to advance the money for a security deposit. Offer advice as to what local apartment projects are doing to attract tenants. With many aggressively seeking new tenants, they are likely to waive a security deposit or give the first month's rent free, which works out to the same thing. Some places will let a tenant make payments over three months until the deposit is paid.

I can't afford to move my stuff.

This problem isn't going to get any better as time passes, so it has to be addressed immediately. Have available a list of moving truck rental places. Lots of large moving companies have employees who work on the side, with their employer's permission, on an hourly basis. The reason you want people from large moving companies is because a small, crosstown move is too small for them, so they don't mind their employees doing it on the side. Printers, quick-copy stores, and libraries usually give away clean boxes.

I have too much stuff and it won't fit anyplace else.

That's why there's self-storage. It's a booming industry and people are building them everywhere. As a result, there's a lot of competition. Especially with brand new facilities, which you make think you couldn't afford, you can move in with the first month or two free as a lease-up incentive.

I'm sentimentally attached to this place.

It's understandable, of course, but shouldn't get in the way of making prudent decisions. On the other hand, this isn't a real rational time for the owner facing foreclosure. Empathize with them and involve them in your plans. Every homeowner has unfinished business in his or her house—repairs that never got done or improvements planned for but never made. Find out those plans and, if possible, incorporate them into your own plans. Allow the owner to take pride in his or her vision and dreams, and your ability to make it come true (even though he or she won't be living there any more).

My dog is buried in the back yard.

Don't laugh! This is a true example. You need to understand that emotional needs are important and offer a variety of ways to meet them. Try a compromise and offer to let him or her dig up selected plants or flowers over the gravesites to take to his or her new residence (under supervision, of course).

I don't want the neighbors to know I've been forced out of my home.

The solution here is to meet that one head-on. Make it seem like a joyful occasion, a successful sale of a property. Once you reach a firm agreement and you know you're going to close, put up a "For Sale" sign in the yard. Wait a few days, and then put up a "Sold" sign. Boy, won't the neighbors be envious then!

I don't want the children to change schools until the end of the year.

Find out the circumstances under which a child can move out of the district and still finish the school year at the old location. School officials are focused on the best interests of the children. There's some latitude and discretion in allowing out-of-district children. As difficult as it might be, explaining about financial problems, loss of the family home, and the emotional impact on a child might persuade a principal to allow the child to finish at the old school.

I'm sure there are more, but you'll get better at this over time. Learn to evaluate people's motivations, practice meeting their true needs without compromising any important ones you might have, and you'll be successful.

> **Insight:**
> If you want to buy a property for your personal residence and the owner wants to remain in the property, I don't recommend letting the former owner stay, for any length of time at all, unless you feel there are just no other options and you really want that particular property.

Keeping the Owner as a Tenant

Sometimes you want the former owner to stay as a tenant, or you feel that you don't have any choice in order to buy the property. Landlord/tenant relations and legal issues can fill up another whole book. My advice is to buy a good book and master the principles in it. Visit with several apartment complexes and get copies of their leases. They'll be good guides for local laws and standard requirements in your community.

For commercial leases, you might need to consult an attorney because the forms are a lot more complicated and have so many different variables depending on the situation. Do your homework before visiting the lawyer so you can be as efficient as possible with him or her. If you live near a law school or a courthouse with a public law library, you might want to visit it and look for landlord/tenant guidebooks.

If you have access to the Internet, search on the following strings. Anyplace you see the word "state," substitute the name of your state.

- landlord tenant law state
- free download house lease
- free download commercial lease

◆ tenant rights state

◆ landlord rights state

There are pros and cons to renting to a former owner. On the upside, former owners give you a ready-made tenant with no loss of income while you clean, paint and change the locks. They generally have pride of ownership even though no longer an owner. Former owners usually stay longer than other tenants, and are the first and best source of buyers if you ever decide to sell.

The cons are the normal downside of being a landlord, but magnified because of the unusual relationship. Former owners feel more free to make *improvements* you might consider objectionable, such as painting the walls black. They sometimes harbor resentment towards you and feel justified in not paying their rent on time. When they move out, they might see nothing wrong with removing the ceiling fans, fancy door knobs, and the refrigerator. Those things can all be handled with a good lease and firm supervision. Other problems require more preparation. They fall into three categories.

1. Landlord liability for defective premises
2. Eviction time and expense
3. Bankruptcy

Landlord Liability for Defective Premises

Generally, landlords are responsible for making sure the premises are safe and livable. There are varying interpretations of what constitutes *livable*. You're not a slum landlord, certainly, but you'd be surprised what a tenant facing eviction will claim about you in order to avoid eviction and possibly collect damages. To help avoid these problems, do the following.

◆ Get the owner/tenant to sign something saying whatever shape the place is in when he or she sells it to you, that's acceptable, and that he or she does not expect you to repair anything unless specifically listed in the lease.

- Keep a diary with the date and substance of any complaints, and what you did to correct any problems. Every time the tenant calls you about a problem, ask them to hold the line while you get your property maintenance diary. That way, they'll know that you're keeping track. It's a good deterrent.
- Maintain a good relationship with your tenant.
- Don't let things slide for too long. A tenant who gets far behind on the rent can't possibly make it up. The only alternative is to walk out, or sue you on some theory. Managing tenants is like managing children—you have to be fair but firm, pay attention, and never get complacent.
- Have good general business liability insurance, naming you, and any corporations or limited liability companies you own, as named insureds on the policy. The fee to include additional insureds is usually nominal, or nothing at all and this protects all your assets.

Eviction Time and Expense

You'll need to know about residential evictions and commercial evictions if you're going to rent to the former owner. Make sure you understand the distinction. Most of the time, consumer evictions are harder to do than business evictions. The law is generally opposed to throwing widows and orphans out on the streets, but doesn't worry so much about sophisticated business people.

Usually, an eviction starts with a notice that gives the tenant a certain amount of days to *cure the default* or get current on the rent. *Default* can also apply to lease violations besides late rent for which the tenant has a right to *cure* (fix). After the cure period expires, the tenant is given an opportunity to vacate the property voluntarily. If he or she doesn't do that, you have to file a lawsuit.

The tenant will have a certain number of days to file an answer and contest your right to reenter the premises and take control of them. A sophisticated tenant can file an answer, demand a trial, and even appeal to a higher court if he or she loses at the trial. Usually they'll claim that something about your purchase was illegal or unethical. The whole process can take longer than you might think, depending on your state. Talk to an attorney or check out consumer and tenant protection websites for more information. Until you get the tenant out, you won't be receiving any rent and there's a high likelihood the tenant is trashing the property.

Remember, though, this is a worst-case situation. You size people up all day long and make decisions regarding what actions you will take, how much you'll trust them, etc. Don't let fear cause you to pass on good opportunities— use your common sense.

Bankruptcy

The three most common types of bankruptcy are Chapter 7, Chapter 11, and Chapter 13. Chapter 7 is a *liquidation*, in which all the debtor's nonexempt assets are sold to pay creditors. The money goes as far as it can go, and, with some rare exceptions involving fraud or taxes, the leftover debts are wiped out. Chapter 13 is available to people who have regular income. It used to be called the *wage-earner's plan*, but you don't have to be a wage earner in order to qualify. You just have to have regular income that can form the basis of a reliable budget.

In Chapter 13, the debtor creates a plan and a budget for paying creditors. Things like rent and mortgage payments have to be made on time after the date of the bankruptcy, but arrearages can be caught up over time.

In a Chapter 11, or *reorganization*, the debtor also proposes a plan but has greater powers to force renegotiation of things like rent and other contracts. Chapter 11 is usually a business bankruptcy.

Bankruptcy is extremely technical. While landlords can do their own evictions, always involve an attorney when dealing with a bankruptcy claim.

Evaluate the Former Owner

Landlord/tenant law is far beyond the scope of this book. Make sure you have a firm grip on the principles, and a good lease form, before you embark on renting to a former owner. Decide on a rental rate that will *at the very least* cover your own mortgage payments, real estate taxes, property insurance, and anticipated repairs. It's not unfair to ask a former owner to pay rent that's a little bit higher than market rents in the area. After all, he or she won't have to go to the trouble and expense of moving, and that has some value.

Be aware that renting to a former owner can be perilous. He or she is already in financial trouble, but it might have been a temporary hole that he or she just couldn't dig out. You're going to have to evaluate for yourself if the tenant can afford the rent.

I recommend you don't take the tenant's word for it, but perform your own analysis using the form on the next page. Ask for proof on all numbers.

Renting to a Former Owner Worksheet

Fixed, recurring expenses each month:

Agreed rent   + _____

Car payments   + _____

Other secured creditors monthly payments (list each one)   + _____

Credit card minimum payments   + _____

Car insurance   + _____

Health insurance   + _____

Other fixed expenses, like child support, alimony, private
school tuition, club dues, church donations, health club,
other mortgages or unsecured notes (list each one)   + _____

Total fixed monthly expenses   =(a) _____

Variable expenses that come up each month or that
can be estimated as an average per month: _____

Gas and auto maintenance   + _____

Food, laundry, medicine   + _____

Average utilities, including cable and Internet   + _____

Entertainment   + _____

Clothing   + _____

Other living expenses (list categories)   + _____

Subtotal variable expenses   =(b) _____

Multiply (b) by 1.1. (This will tell you how much the
variable expenses will be if you add 10% to them for surprises.) =(c) _____

Add (a) and (c) to obtain grand total of monthly expenses   =(d) _____

Tenant's take-home pay (make copies of last three pay stubs
or get written permission to confirm with their employer)   = _____

If the Total Income is not more than the Total Expenses, ask the seller what they are going to do to trim the expenses. Eating less is not an answer. Giving up the health insurance is not an acceptable answer. Not paying other creditors isn't recommended; nor is reducing the 10% cushion for surprises. Resigning from the health club or country club or putting the children in public school are some possibilities.

A seller who can't meet his or her rent obligations under the budget you put together isn't a candidate for a sale and leaseback. If you can't structure the deal so the former owner moves out, then pass on the opportunity. Stretching in order to make it work, and hoping for the best, will almost always turn into disaster.

It might seem like a good idea to go through this exercise with *all* tenants, not just former owners. As a practical matter, though, you won't be able to. There are lots of other landlords out there willing to rent property to prospective tenants. Unless there's something really special about yours, nobody's going to go through the budgeting exercise. In the case of a former owner, however, there is something special about the property—it used to be his or hers. This person is especially motivated to do whatever it takes to stay there.

Problems at Closing

Occasionally, you'll work with a seemingly reasonable seller with no desire to remain in the property, and then be surprised after closing when you can't get them out. Some experts advise you not to close until the seller vacates the property. It's good advice, but usually not real world. Most of the time, a seller won't leave until they're sure the deal is going through, but *you* can't be absolutely sure its going to happen until you reach the closing table.

To address those concerns, you need to take away all the back doors that let you wiggle out of a contract if something unexpected turns up. It's called making the contract *go hard*. You can accomplish this with a simple letter telling the seller that all contingencies have been removed and you are prepared to proceed to closing. A savvy seller may also demand a commitment letter from the bank saying they'll finance you *and* proof that your down payment had been escrowed and was available. Lots of people have good intentions, but then can't close because they can't get the money.

If you have no desire to keep the seller as a tenant, and he or she has no desire to stay, ask him or her to vacate before closing. If you meet resistance, find out his or her true fears and try to calm them with something more than soothing words.

Manage the Move

You can avoid a lot of eviction problems by shepherding the move process. A seller who agrees to move on March 1, for example, probably should start packing up their house around mid-February. Look for signs of packing. Ask for the new address. Monitor the situation to make sure he or she is really working on moving. If it comes down to closing day and you see no signs of moving, no firm plans for a new place to live or work, and no indication anybody's doing anything, then you should be alarmed. Delay closing three days and tell the seller to get out, or you won't proceed. I recommend a contract clause that say something like the following:

> *Closing is scheduled on or before _____. Seller will vacate the property by 4:00 pm, Central Time, on the 3rd day after closing. If Buyer reasonably believes that Seller will not be able to meet its commitment regarding vacating, then Buyer may close into escrow, pending Seller's timely vacation. If Seller fails to vacate by the date and time required, then this contract shall, at Buyer's option, be void and Buyer will be entitled to a complete refund of all monies.*

If it comes down to it and you have to do an eviction, then start immediately. A seller who told you he or she would move out within three days of closing, and then reneges, can't be trusted. This might sound cold, but he or she has already defaulted on the mortgage payments. Now he or she is not meeting his or her commitments to you. Don't listen to any sad stories at this point. Start your eviction proceeding immediately. You're not throwing stuff out on the street, you're beginning a legal process that will take a few weeks even if everything goes well. There's simply no point in delaying.

Most states have guides regarding the eviction process for their jurisdiction. You can find these by visiting consumer protection agencies, law schools, county law libraries, or perhaps even office supply stores. Some of the more populous states even have complete books you can buy regarding landlord/tenancy law, including evictions.

On the Internet, search the string *"eviction forms state,"* except use the name of your state for the word "state."

Don't be afraid to rent your property to the former owner. Armed with knowledge regarding the law, a strong lease, and a good adherence to systems and procedures to monitor things before they turn into problems, you'll do well.

20

Tax Considerations

Unfortunately, Uncle Sam has a vested interest in your foreclosure purchase plans. He wants to nab his share. You want to keep as much as possible. Knowing some tax law will give you an advantage in the battle.

Tax issues fall into several categories. The main concerns generally include:

- expenses that are deductible immediately;
- expenses that have to be deducted over the course of several years (depreciation);
- annual income taxes;
- how much tax will I have to pay on a sale; and,
- how can I delay paying taxes until some time in the distant future.

Deductions

Deductions are fairly simple. Do your homework and keep good records. Homework means learning enough tax law to know, for example, replacing half a roof is a deductible expense right now, but replacing a whole roof has to be deducted over a long period of time. Keeping good records allows you to deduct everything remotely related to the property and its management.

That's all pretty standard stuff and is covered in any good book on owning rental properties.

Depreciation

Depreciation lets you deduct the value of the improvements on your income producing property over some period of time. Currently, the IRS is of the opinion that residential rental properties will wear out in 27.5 years, but commercial properties will wear out over the course of 39 years. You can deduct a portion of that each year, as a depreciation deduction.

Income Taxes During Ownership

Many people will tell you that you can lose money every month on a piece of rental property, but still come out ahead because of the tax deductions. This used to be true, when the IRS allowed some very aggressive types of depreciation accounting over short time periods. Now, largely, such advice is urban legend. One example will illustrate the mechanics of depreciation deductions and how little money they actually save the average investor.

The post office Jim was considering purchasing would have resulted in a negative cash flow for him, as follows.

Post Office: Cash Flow Analysis

Gross Annual Rents	+12,000
Potential Vacancies	-0
Landlord Expenses	-2,000
Net Operating Income	=10,000
Annual Mortgage Payments	-11,511
Cash Flow	($1,511)

There's a negative cash flow of $1,511 per year.

The same property, with the taxable income calculations results in a very different picture. Taxable income will add a depreciation expenses that doesn't affect cash flow. Any potential vacancies would not be expensed; actual vacancies would diminish income, though. For tax purposes, only the interest portion of the annual mortgage expense is deductible, not the entire mortgage payment. Depreciation is $1/39^{th}$ of the improvement portion of the purchase price. Just because Jim could buy the Post Office building for $200,000, doesn't mean he takes depreciation on the entire amount. Some portion of the purchase price was for land, which can't be depreciated. We arbitrarily allocated $50,000 to land and $150,000 to improvements—the building, parking lot, driveways, etc.

Post Office: Cash Flow Analysis

Gross Annual Rents	+12,000
Potential Vacancies	Irrelevant
Landlord Expenses	-2,000
Depreciation Expense (1/39 of $150,000)	-3,846
First year's interest payment	-3,195
Taxable Income	$2,959

There's a tax profit of $2,959 in the first year!

That's the truth to the urban legend of real estate losses being more than offset by tax savings. In the example above, Jim had negative cash flow of $1,511 in the first year. But, he has to report a profit to the IRS of $2,959, *and pay taxes on it*. If Jim's in the 15% tax bracket, then the paper profit he made will cost him another $443.85 in taxes. Instead of saving money on his taxes, Jim had to pay additional taxes.

You don't need to be scared of taxes, though. Do your calculations, know what you're getting into, and make informed decisions.

Income Taxes on Home Sales

Tax rates at the time of sale depend on whether the property is your personal residence, and on how long you've owned it. Under current law, homeowners can sell their personal residence and make up to $250,000 profit per owner, tax free.

Taxes are imposed on profits. To diminish profits as much as possible, you want to be able to demonstrate that you've spent lots of money after the initial purchase, just in case the tax laws change.

Repairs don't count towards reducing your profit, but *capital improvements* do. A whole new roof is a capital improvement. A roof repair isn't. Converting the garage to a family room is a capital improvement. Keep records of all the money you spend in case you ever need to let an accountant figure it out when and if the tax laws change.

Calculating Taxable Profits on Commercial Properties

For commercial properties, all of your *profit* is taxable, but you might be surprised how profit is calculated. That's because of depreciation. Owners of commercial properties are able to deduct depreciation on their taxes returns each year, but the deduction does come back later.

Example: Let's say Jim buys the Post Office, for example, for $200,000. First, he has to allocate the purchase price between land and improvements. We'll say that the land is worth $50,000 and the improvements are worth $150,000. Every year, Jim can deduct 1/39th of $150,000, or $3,846 as an expense on his income taxes. That *shelters* $3,846 worth of cash income on which Jim doesn't have to pay taxes.

Let's assume he owns the Post Office for five years, and then for some strange reason sells it for only $210,000. Jim's purchase price is called his *basis*. The depreciation deductions he takes each year reduce his basis by the same amount. Five years worth of depreciation deductions total $19,230. For purposes of calculating IRS profit, Jim has to subtract

$19,230 from his $200,000 purchase price. That gives him an adjusted basis of $180,770. This makes sense if you think about the fact that Jim's already received the benefit of $19,230 in tax savings. He doesn't get to receive them twice.

He has to take his sales price of $210,000 and subtract his adjusted basis of $180,770 to arrive at an IRS profit of $29,230. This is the amount on which he owes taxes.

The amount of taxes depends on how he characterizes the $29,230, and how long he's owned the property. Some of the $29,230 actually represents depreciation benefits he used in the past and then *recaptured*, to use an IRS term. That amount is taxed at one rate. The balance is taxed at different rates depending on Jim's tax bracket and whether the property qualifies for short-term, long-term, or super long-term tax benefits. The calculations are beyond the scope of this book and you should seek professional tax advice if you are in this situation. However, you need to always consider the tax aspects of what you are going to do so you can plan accordingly.

Deferring Taxes

I know lots of people who want to buy property, but fear reselling it because the taxes would wipe them out. I always tell them about a little-known loophole that sophisticated investors use all the time. It's called a *1031 exchange* (pronounced "ten thirty-one exchange").

Section 1031 of the Internal Revenue Code is one of the best kept secrets in the world. Basically, it says that *if you do everything exactly by the IRS rules* you can sell property at a profit and not pay any taxes until years later.

You heard me right—sell property at a profit, put money in your pocket, and pay NO taxes right now. The *right now* obviously means that you will have to pay the tax eventually, but that could be decades later. The *later* could be when you are in a lower tax bracket, when you might qualify for better capital gains rates, or, best of all, you might be dead and it'll be your kids problem. The IRS is going to get theirs, eventually. The trick is to put it off as long as possible.

Taking advantage of Section 1031 is technical, but not difficult. You should refer to more in-depth discussions than I can give you here. In a nutshell, though, here are the requirements:

◆ Sell Property #1.

◆ Make sure that a 1031 agent (usually the closing attorney) takes all the money from the sale and puts it in his or her escrow account. Your fingers can *never* touch the money.

◆ Fill out a form in which you *identify* (describe with some particularity) a *like-kind* property you plan to buy within forty-five days of the sale.

◆ Invest all of your Property #1 *equity* into Property #2 within 180 days of the sale of Property #1.

Insight

If you have property *for sale*, and you know that another investor's *1031 clock is ticking*, then you know that he desperately needs to buy something else, quickly. He's a great prospect to buy your property, and will generally pay a somewhat higher price because of all the taxes he's saving.

◆ Finally, report the 1031 exchange on your tax return. The taxes become due when you quit *rolling over* your equity into new properties, and finally *cash-out*.

There's one major wrinkle—you have to hold the properties for investment. That means you can't be *flipping* them all the time, or buying and selling within very short time periods. There are some *safe harbor* ways to make sure you always qualify as an investor, but they are outside the scope of this book. Even with these technicalities, a 1031 exchange is fairly sample and a great way to defer taxes possibly indefinitely.

21

Go Out and Be a Hero

The tools you've gained from this book give you x-ray vision to analyze opportunities, lightning speed to eliminate rejects immediately, and super-human strength to concentrate your efforts where they will bring the highest rewards. You already have the moral and ethical predisposition to be a hero. People facing foreclosure desperately need you to help solve their problems and to save them from the multitude of predatory foreclosure experts.

Most people facing foreclosure are resigned to losing their property. They want other things—respect, plans for the future, an orderly transition, lack of embarrassment, and preservation of a credit score. You can provide that. Sometimes they want to avoid complete loss of their equity. My techniques plus your creative thinking, can make that possible in many instances and still earn you a tidy profit.

You're ready. Go out and be a hero! The country doesn't have enough heroes in the realm of foreclosure purchasing, and we need all the ones we can find.

Glossary

A

adverse possession (squatter's rights). Under some circumstances, some-one who uses your land for ten or twenty years (depending on the state and some technical details) and acts as if it's their own property, can take it away from you.

agent. Someone who represents someone else and can, under some circum-stances, bind them to contracts. Real estate agents typically represent the sellers, even if they are "working with" you. Always ask who the agent repre-sents. They might not have your best interests at heart!

appreciation. In the real world, most real estate grows in value over the years, or appreciates.

C

capitalization method. A method of estimating the value of income producing property by calculating the Net Operating Income and then assigning a Cap Rate. The Net Operating Income divided by the Cap Rate gives you an estimate of value.

cash flowing. A property is "cash flowing" when you're able to put money in the bank each month.

certificate of occupancy. Certificate from a government department, usually the Inspections Department, approving a building for use. If you do not obtain a certificate of occupancy when one is required, you can be prohibited from using your property, or renting it out to anyone else.

comparables method. A method of estimating value by comparing the subject property to similar properties that have sold in the recent past.

C-paper. Loans to people with low credit scores or other risk factors; usually at much-higher than typical interest rates.

C-store. A convenience store.

D

deed of trust. A security instrument by which real estate secures a promissory note. In some states, this is arrangement is a slightly different document, called a mortgage.

deferred maintenance. Repairs that have been put off for awhile and are starting to pile up.

deficiency. The money a borrower might still owe their lender after a foreclosure.

depreciation. An accounting concept in which the IRS, and other people, pretend that assets will decrease steadily in value over a predetermined time period until, at the very end, they are completely worthless. It usually bears no relationship to reality, but does allow you to write off expenses on your taxes even though you're not actually writing checks for those expenses.

distressed property. A polite way of referring to a property owner facing foreclosure.

due diligence. All the research you should do to satisfy yourself that your purchase is as safe as possible.

duress. Some extraneous pressure that causes people to sell property cheaply (because they're facing foreclosure) or causes other people to pay an unusually high price (in order to avoid income taxes).

E

eminent domain. The ability of the government to take property, whether the homeowner wants to sell or not. Until recently, eminent domain powers were used to acquire land for schools, roads and similar things. In 2005, the United States Supreme Court held that governments can use eminent domain to acquire land in order to develop it into shopping centers that would add to the tax revenues.

equity. The difference between what a property is worth and what is owed on it. Just because someone pays $10,000 down to buy a property, doesn't mean they still have $10,000 in equity. If the property appreciated—or grew in value—then the equity will be larger. If the property declined in value, then the equity will be smaller.

F

fair market value (FMV). The price that a willing buyer would pay a willing seller, with neither of them operating under duress.

J

joint tenants. A method of property ownership. If a joint tenant sells their share to someone else, it destroys the joint tenancy and turns it into a tenancy in common. If a joint tenant dies, his share is split equally among the surviving joint tenants.

judicial foreclosure. Obtaining a court order in order to foreclose on real estate. This is required in some states.

L

lien. A generic name for claims against real estate. Lienholders can hold mortgages, they can be creditors who filed judgments, or they might be taxing authorities like the IRS or your local government.

lis pendens. A notice placed in the real estate records that someone has a claim against property, even though that claim might not rise to the status of a lien. Heirs fighting over property might file lis pendens notices against each other. Spouses in the process of a divorce not yet finalized might file a lis pendens in order to put potential purchasers or lienholders that someone else might own the property before too long, and all buyers should beware!

M

mechanics and materialmen's lien (M&M liens). This is a lien that suppliers and workers can place on property for the value of their goods and services.

mortgage. A security instrument by which real estate secures a promissory note. In some states, this is arrangement is a slightly different document, called a deed of trust.

N

negative cash flow. Assuming you make all your bank deposits on time, and pay all your bills on time, you have negative cash flow when there's not enough money in the bank to pay your bills.

nonjudicial foreclosure. Being able to foreclose on real estate without a court's assistance. This is allowed in some states.

O

owned real estate (ORE). Sometimes called REO (Real Estate-Owned). This is the portfolio of property on which a bank has foreclosed and still owns. Technically, branch banks would seem to be "owned real estate" but the term refers only to foreclosure properties.

P

priority. A method of ranking lienholders to determine who gets the first money off the top on a sale, who gets the second money, and so on. Except for very specialized circumstances in a bankruptcy, lienholders do not share money pro-rata. Each one must be paid in full before you can go to the next lower, or "junior" lienholder.

profit. What you pay taxes on. Because the principal portion of mortgage payments don't qualify as an accounting or an IRS expense, you can have a paper profit but still not have enough money to pay your bills.

T

tenancy by the entireties. A method of property ownership for husbands and wives. One spouse is not allowed to sell their share unless both of them agree. No one, not even a divorce court, can take the property away from just one owner. If one spouse dies, the other one inherits that share.

tenants in common. A method of property ownership. Tenants in common share property, but no one has a particular piece. A tenant in common can sell their share to someone else. If a tenant in common dies, their heirs inherit their share.

title binder. This is not title insurance. The binder says that if you do all the things the title company requires—like paying the purchase money and recording a deed—then they will issue title insurance when you pay the premium. A title binder is worthless if you don't complete all the steps and pay the premium.

title insurance. An insurance policy that pays off if it turns out that you don't have good and clear title to your property. Title insurance typically does not cover boundary line disputes or adverse possession claims. Lenders always require title insurance, but many buyers don't think to ask for coverage for themselves, also. That would be similar to buying car insurance that pays just GMAC if you wreck the car.

torrens. A method of registering the owner of real estate and all liens against the property. It is similar to a car title. Torrens systems are voluntary. They are allowed in some counties, in some states.

triple net lease. A landlord/tenant arrangement in which the tenant pays all the expenses of property ownership, such as taxes, insurance and maintenance. This is very common with commercial leases, and extremely uncommon with residential leases.

U

unlawful detainer. Legalese for an eviction lawsuit.

upper bracket. Real estate agent's way of referring to upper middle class, but not fabulously wealthy, people.

W

write-down. A lender agreeing to take less than the full debt as payment in full.

Appendix: Understanding the Real Estate Contract

Using a real estate contract when purchasing a property is crucial. It defines your agreement and can both protect you from a situation gone bad, and be used to assert your position when dealing with a seller. You should buy some real estate contracts from your local office supply store, or download some from the Internet, and review them for clauses that might be important to you.

The form provided here explains the various clauses contained in a standard contract.

All sellers should be listed here, not just the person you're negotiating with. You should put your personal name in the blank as the purchaser. Another clause in the contract will let you assign the contract to any company in which you are a partner or shareholder.

Many times a real estate contract must include the legal description of the property in order to be enforceable. On the other hand, you sometimes don't know the legal description at such an early stage. To avoid misunderstandings, include as much information as you have, including the general description of the property. As general description might be one of the following: *The Seller's principal residence* or *A small office building at the corner of Oak Street and Fifth Avenue* or something similar. Be aware that street addresses and general descriptions can be misleading. A house might have one street address, but include

Contract to Buy and Sell Real Property

Parties. The Seller is _____

_____.

The Purchaser is _____

_____.

The Seller agrees to sell and the Purchaser agrees to buy the property described below.

Property. The street address of the property is _____

_____,

in the City/Town of _____,

County/Parish of _____,

the State of _____.

It is generally described as _____

_____

_____

_____.

A legal description will be added later to this contract. The Property includes all improvements, shrubbery, plantings, fixtures, and appurtenances.

Purchase Price. The purchase price will be $_____, payable as follows:

Earnest Money. Purchaser has given the following escrow agent _____ _____ a check in the amount of $_____ as earnest money. It will be used as a credit against the full purchase price. In the event Purchaser fails to go through

two complete subdivision lots, with the additional lot having its own address. Or, a rental house with a detached garage apartment could have two separate addresses. When in doubt, use as many words as necessary to spell out what you're buying, and then add the legal description as soon as possible afterwards. Be sure that all parties initial the legal description.

Don't be afraid to spell out exactly how the deal is going to be structured. If the purchase is $70,000, payable by payment directly to the lender, then say so. If it includes splitting the profits of a resale, with 80% going to you and 20% to the seller, then describe how you'll calculate whether there's a profit or not, and how large. Even if you have to include an entire worksheet by way of example, do so. It's better to be wordy and clear, than succinct and vague.

It is unusual for a foreclosure purchase to include earnest money. If you're forced to put up earnest money by the lender or a seller with many interested buyers, then remember that this seller is in trouble. Don't give him or her the earnest money to keep. Pay the small fee, and name an escrow agent. It could be the lender itself, an attorney, or a title company.

This clause protects you because it forces the seller to disclose property defects. It also protects the seller because it gives him or her a safe harbor—as long as he or she discloses, you, the purchaser, assume the risk that the repairs might be more expensive than originally anticipated.

with closing for any reason, except Seller's refusal or inability to close, or one of the contingencies listed below, Seller may be paid the earnest money as liquidated damages and Purchaser will have no further liability to Seller. Seller may market the property until the date of closing and may accept "backup contracts" in order to mitigate its damages in the event Purchaser refuses or fails to proceed with closing.

Property Accepted "As Is." Purchaser is familiar with the property and any defects or problems it might have. Purchaser is accepting the property *as is* and will not hold Seller responsible for any repairs that are necessary after closing, as long as they've been generally disclosed here:

Contingencies. Purchaser's obligation to buy depends on its satisfaction that the following contingencies have been removed:

Title Insurance. Purchaser's obligation to buy depends on being able to secure title insurance at closing, showing that Purchaser has clear and marketable title to the property free of any liens or encumbrances (except as may be accepted by Purchaser in writing). If Seller is unable to deliver clear and marketable title, as evidenced by title insurance, then Purchaser may elect to declare this contract null and void, even if all time periods have expired for other contingencies and even if Purchaser has stated that it will proceed to closing.

List here *anything* you might require before you're willing to completely obligate yourself to buying the property. Sample contingencies might be something as vague as: *Completion of all due diligence deemed reasonably necessary by Purchaser, in its sole discretion,* or as specific as, *Written confirmation from lender that it will accept a write-down of its debt to $70,000* and *Seller's ability to transfer title free and clear of any and all claims or liens.*

Foreclosure properties present unusual risks, including the high risk that someone could record a lien at the last minute. That's why title insurance should be addressed as a completely separate contingency—you can't be sure you're safe until you reach the closing table and receive the title insurance policy.

This clause avoids all the open-ended abuses rampant in foreclosure sales. Typically, the purchaser has all the flexibility and the seller has no choice except to keep his or her fingers crossed and hope there's a closing before there's a foreclosure. Under this proposed paragraph, the parties agree on a time limit for the purchaser to do his or her due diligence. When the time limit arrives, the purchaser has to go *on the record* and declare his or her intentions. If the purchaser does nothing, then the seller can either force a sale or declare the contract void (at the seller's option). The seller also has to go *on the record* and give notice of his election. If neither party does anything, the contract is null and void. Typically, if the due diligence takes longer than originally anticipated, the parties should meet and agree on an amendment, changing the date for removal of contingencies.

Time Limit for Removal of Contingencies. Purchaser must notify Seller by _____ whether it is proceeding to closing or not, and that all contingencies have been removed if it is proceeding to closing. Notice must be in writing and there must be some sort of proof of delivery to Seller at the following address: _____

_____ .

Failure to give the required notice will result in Seller having the option to require Purchaser to proceed to closing, or declare the contract null and void. Seller may exercise his or her option, either to proceed or not, by delivering a notice to Purchaser by _____,
at the following address: _____

_____

_____ .

Notice must be in writing and there must be proof of delivery to Seller. If

Seller does not give any notice by the required time limit, this contract will be null and void.

There needs to be a deadline for closing, so the parties know if there's a default or not. If the purchaser has no time limit for closing, he or she could continue to *hang out*, claiming that he or she has every intention of buying the property, until foreclosure renders that impossible.

Closing. Closing will take place on or within one week afterwards.

This clause isn't included for the purposes of *flipping* a contract. It's here to let you sign a contract with the seller and then figure out later if you want the property owned personally, or in the name of a corporation or some other legal entity. If you're intent on flipping properties, then delete the last part of the sentence that reads "...in which he or she holds a legal or beneficial interest."

Assignment. Purchaser may assign this contract to any company, corporation, partnership, LLC, trust, or any other legal entity in which he or she holds a legal or beneficial interest.

Risk of Loss; Insurance. Until closing takes place, Seller will be responsible for keeping the property adequately insured and for making any repairs. After closing, Purchaser will be responsible for all insurance and repairs. If Seller fails to

One would hope the seller has property insurance, but that's not always the case. Ask for proof of insurance. Have yourself named as an additional insured, so you'll get notice if the insurance is cancelled. If the seller doesn't have property insurance, ask your insurance agency if you can bind coverage for a nominal sum. Under no circumstances should you loan the borrower the money to buy insurance.

Try to find out all the normal closing costs in your area. If this is a no-equity purchase, the seller probably can't afford to pay anything at all. If it's a deferred payment for equity situation in which the seller will receive some money in the future, then spell out how the seller will pay his or her portion of the closing costs. Maybe he or she will need to bring cash to the closing table. Maybe you'll pay all the closing expenses but the seller will reimburse you through a deduction from any money you'll owe him or her in the future. If you're buying from a bank's ORE department, try to get them to pay all closing costs. Usually, you'll be successful.

maintain sufficient insurance and there is an uninsured or underinsured loss, Purchaser may elect to purchase the property or to declare this contract null and void. In the event of a casualty loss, Purchaser may extend the closing date, the contingency removal date, or both by a reasonable time to evaluate the extent of the damage and the adequacy of insurance coverage.

Closing Costs. Seller will pay:

½ of title policy

½ of attorney's fees

Purchaser will pay:

½ of title policy

½ of attorney's fees

All recording/filing fees

Possession. Seller (and anyone claiming under Seller or allowed to remain in possession by Seller—all of whom will be called "Seller" in this paragraph) will vacate the premises by _____ _____. If Purchaser has reason to believe that Seller will not honor its agreement to vacate by the above date, then Purchaser may close into escrow and await evidence that Seller has vacated. If Seller has not vacated by the agreed date, then Purchaser will have the option to declare this contract null and void, or it may proceed with final closing and evict Seller. In addition, if Seller has not vacated by the agreed date but the Purchaser elects to proceed with final closing, Purchaser's damages and/or costs of eviction may be deducted from any sums to become due to Seller.

Getting the former owner out of the property can be a major headache. This clause allows the Purchaser a *wait and see* time period. It also covers the situation in which the bank is the seller but the former owner is still in possession. Make it the bank's problem to get the former owner out.

You must check your state law for the required waiting periods and for any warnings or other disclosures that must appear in contracts with sellers facing foreclosure. As written, this clause makes it clear that you aren't placing pressure on the seller to sign immediately, but honestly desire that he or she make a decision only after considering all of his or her options and their consequences.

Make sure all sellers sign. Have a third-party witness their signatures—not you. If they sign outside your presence, obtain the names and addresses of the witnesses and call them to confirm their signatures. Foreclosure is a tense, emotional time, and people sometimes do strange things. Don't take any chances. For states like California, with strong consumer protection laws in place, you might even require that the seller's signature be notarized. Whatever you do, don't witness or notarize the signatures yourself. You're an interested party and should not be a witness or notary.

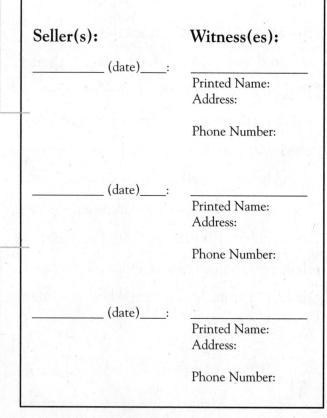

Cooling Off Period. Seller has been given _____ days to consider this contract, discuss it with any advisors, and negotiate any of the terms. The resulting contract, signed by the parties, has been entered into after full deliberation and negotiation and is the full and complete agreement of the parties.

Seller(s):   **Witness(es):**

_____ (date)____: _____

                                     Printed Name:
                                     Address:

                                     Phone Number:

_____ (date)____: _____

                                     Printed Name:
                                     Address:

                                     Phone Number:

_____ (date)____: _____

                                     Printed Name:
                                     Address:

                                     Phone Number:

Index

I

J

L

M

N

Uniform Residential Mortgage
    Foreclosure Act, 204
upper limit price, 198
utilities, 131, 144, 146, 153, 164,
    168, 169, 219

W

wage-earner's plan, 217
Waiver of Confidentiality and
    Request for Information, 107
warehouses, 21
workout departments, 52, 53
workout specialist, 2, 3, 4, 8, 62, 63,
    65, 67, 68, 76, 96
write-downs, 126, 179, 180, 194

Z

zoning, 129

About the Author

Denise L. Evans received her law degree from the University of Alabama Law School, with a concentration in real estate, tax, and finance. While a law student, she served on the Board of Editors for the Journal of the Legal Profession, published two scholarly articles, was Director of the Legal Research Department, and clerked with a law firm that had a large real estate practice. She graduated at the top of her class, earning the prestigious Henderson M. Somerville Prize. Afterwards, she spent several years in Houston, Texas in commercial litigation, much of it real estate-related. At the pinnacle of her legal career, she headed a specialized department of eight litigation attorneys and support staff, and conducted legal training for lawyers throughout south Texas.

Today, she is a successful business woman in a variety of real estate-related businesses, including one which she sold several years ago for a profit of several million dollars. She is a licensed commercial real estate broker with a very active practice. She has twenty years of experience in conducting seminars, consulting, and passing on her secrets and insights to other people, as well as successfully implementing them herself. Ms. Evans has implemented, tested, and proven all of the concepts in *How to Make Money on Foreclosures*.

Never content to rest on her laurels, she applied for, and was accepted as, a candidate for the coveted CCIM (Certified Commercial Investment Member) designation. Ms. Evans serves on the finance committee of the Birmingham chapter of CREW (Commercial Real Estate Women) and is a research associate for the Alabama Real Estate Research and Education Center at the University of Alabama. She organized a very successful merchants' association for her part of town, and serves as President.

She resides with her husband, two Chinese Pugs, a German Shepherd, half a million honey bees (really!) and assorted wildlife on forty acres of relatively blissful peace on Lake Tuscaloosa, in Alabama.

SPHINX® PUBLISHING'S STATE TITLES

Up-to-Date for Your State

California Titles

How to File for Divorce in CA (5E)	$26.95
How to Settle & Probate an Estate in CA (2E)	$28.95
How to Start a Business in CA (2E)	$21.95
How to Win in Small Claims Court in CA (2E)	$18.95
Landlords' Legal Guide in CA (2E)	$24.95
Make Your Own CA Will	$18.95
Tenants' Rights in CA	$21.95

Florida Titles

Child Custody, Visitation and Support in FL	$26.95
How to File for Divorce in FL (8E)	$28.95
How to Form a Corporation in FL (6E)	$24.95
How to Form a Limited Liability Co. in FL (3E)	$24.95
How to Form a Partnership in FL	$22.95
How to Make a FL Will (7E)	$16.95
How to Probate and Settle an Estate in FL (5E)	$26.95
How to Start a Business in FL (7E)	$21.95
How to Win in Small Claims Court in FL (7E)	$18.95
Land Trusts in Florida (7E)	$29.95
Landlords' Rights and Duties in FL (9E)	$22.95

Georgia Titles

How to File for Divorce in GA (5E)	$21.95
How to Start a Business in GA (4E)	$21.95

Illinois Titles

Child Custody, Visitation and Support in IL	$24.95
How to File for Divorce in IL (3E)	$24.95
How to Make an IL Will (3E)	$16.95
How to Start a Business in IL (4E)	$21.95
Landlords' Legal Guide in IL	$24.95

Maryland, Virginia and the District of Columbia Titles

How to File for Divorce in MD, VA, and DC	$28.95
How to Start a Business in MD, VA, or DC	$21.95

Massachusetts Titles

How to Form a Corporation in MA	$24.95
How to Start a Business in MA (4E)	$21.95
Landlords' Legal Guide in MA (2E)	$24.95

Michigan Titles

How to File for Divorce in MI (4E)	$24.95
How to Make a MI Will (3E)	$16.95
How to Start a Business in MI (4E)	$24.95

California Titles

How to File for Divorce in CA (5E)	$26.95
How to Settle & Probate an Estate in CA (2E)	$28.95
How to Start a Business in CA (2E)	$21.95
How to Win in Small Claims Court in CA (2E)	$18.95
Landlords' Legal Guide in CA (2E)	$24.95
Make Your Own CA Will	$18.95
Tenants' Rights in CA	$21.95

Florida Titles

Child Custody, Visitation and Support in FL	$26.95
How to File for Divorce in FL (8E)	$28.95
How to Form a Corporation in FL (6E)	$24.95
How to Form a Limited Liability Co. in FL (3E)	$24.95
How to Form a Partnership in FL	$22.95
How to Make a FL Will (7E)	$16.95
How to Probate and Settle an Estate in FL (5E)	$26.95
How to Start a Business in FL (7E)	$21.95
How to Win in Small Claims Court in FL (7E)	$18.95
Land Trusts in Florida (7E)	$29.95
Landlords' Rights and Duties in FL (9E)	$22.95

Georgia Titles

How to File for Divorce in GA (5E)	$21.95
How to Start a Business in GA (4E)	$21.95

Illinois Titles

Child Custody, Visitation and Support in IL	$24.95
How to File for Divorce in IL (3E)	$24.95
How to Make an IL Will (3E)	$16.95
How to Start a Business in IL (4E)	$21.95
Landlords' Legal Guide in IL	$24.95

Maryland, Virginia and the District of Columbia Titles

How to File for Divorce in MD, VA, and DC	$28.95
How to Start a Business in MD, VA, or DC	$21.95

Massachusetts Titles

How to Form a Corporation in MA	$24.95
How to Start a Business in MA (4E)	$21.95
Landlords' Legal Guide in MA (2E)	$24.95

Michigan Titles

How to File for Divorce in MI (4E)	$24.95
How to Make a MI Will (3E)	$16.95
How to Start a Business in MI (4E)	$24.95

SPHINX® PUBLISHING'S NATIONAL TITLES
Valid in All 50 States

LEGAL SURVIVAL IN BUSINESS

The Complete Book of Corporate Forms (2E)	$29.95
The Complete Hiring and Firing Handbook	$19.95
The Complete Limited Liability Company Kit	$24.95
The Complete Partnership Book	$24.95
The Complete Patent Book	$26.95
The Entrepreneur's Internet Handbook	$21.95
The Entrepreneur's Legal Guide	$26.95
Financing Your Small Business	$17.95
Fired, Laid-Off or Forced Out	$14.95
How to Buy a Franchise	$19.95
How to Form a Nonprofit Corporation (3E)	$24.95
How to Form Your Own Corporation (4E)	$26.95
How to Register Your Own Copyright (5E)	$24.95
HR for Small Business	$14.95
Incorporate in Delaware from Any State	$26.95
Incorporate in Nevada from Any State	$24.95
The Law (In Plain English)® for Small Business	$19.95
The Law (In Plain English)® for Writers	$14.95
Making Music Your Business	$18.95
Minding Her Own Business (4E)	$14.95
Most Valuable Business Legal Forms You'll Ever Need (3E)	$21.95
Profit from Intellectual Property	$28.95
Protect Your Patent	$24.95
The Small Business Owner's Guide to Bankruptcy	$21.95
Tax Power for the Self-Employed	$17.95
Tax Smarts for Small Business	$21.95
Your Rights at Work	$14.95

LEGAL SURVIVAL IN COURT

Attorney Responsibilities & Client Rights	$19.95
Crime Victim's Guide to Justice (2E)	$21.95
Legal Research Made Easy (3E)	$21.95
Winning Your Personal Injury Claim (3E)	$24.95

LEGAL SURVIVAL IN REAL ESTATE

The Complete Kit to Selling Your Own Home	$18.95
Essential Guide to Real Estate Contracts (2E)	$18.95
Essential Guide to Real Estate Leases	$18.95
Homeowner's Rights	$19.95
How to Buy a Condominium or Townhome (2E)	$19.95
How to Buy Your First Home (2E)	$14.95
How to Make Money on Foreclosures	$16.95
The Mortgage Answer Book	$14.95
The Weekend Landlord	$16.95
Working with Your Homeowners Association	$19.95

LEGAL SURVIVAL IN SPANISH

Cómo Comprar su Primera Casa	$8.95
Cómo Conseguir Trabajo en los Estados Unidos	$8.95
Cómo Hacer su Propio Testamento	$16.95
Cómo Negociar su Crédito	$8.95
Cómo Organizar un Presupuesto	$8.95
Cómo Solicitar su Propio Divorcio	$24.95
Guía de Inmigración a Estados Unidos (4E)	$24.95
Guía de Justicia para Víctimas del Crimen	$21.95
Guía Esencial para los Contratos de Arrendamiento de Bienes Raices	$22.95
	$16.95
Inmigración y Ciudadanía en los EE.UU. Preguntas y Respuestas	
Inmigración a los EE.UU. Paso a Paso (2E)	$24.95
Manual de Beneficios del Seguro Social	$18.95
El Seguro Social Preguntas y Respuestas	$16.95
¡Visas! ¡Visas! ¡Visas!	$9.95

Legal Survival in Personal Affairs

101 Complaint Letters That Get Results	$18.95
The 529 College Savings Plan (2E)	$18.95
The 529 College Savings Plan Made Simple	$7.95
The Alternative Minimum Tax	$14.95
The Antique and Art Collector's Legal Guide	$24.95
The Childcare Answer Book	$12.95
Child Support	$18.95
The Complete Adoption and Fertility Legal Guide	$24.95
The Complete Book of Insurance	$18.95
The Complete Book of Personal Legal Forms	$24.95
The Complete Credit Repair Kit	$18.95
The Complete Legal Guide to Senior Care	$21.95
Credit Smart	$18.95
The Easy Will and Living Will Kit	$16.95
Fathers' Rights	$19.95
The Frequent Traveler's Guide	$14.95
File Your Own Divorce (6E)	$24.95
Gay & Lesbian Rights	$26.95
Grandparents' Rights (3E)	$24.95
How to File Your Own Bankruptcy (6E)	$21.95
How to Make Your Own Simple Will (3E)	$18.95
How to Parent with Your Ex	$12.95
How to Write Your Own Living Will (4E)	$18.95
How to Write Your Own Premarital Agreement (3E)	$24.95
Law 101	$16.95
Law School 101	$16.95
The Living Trust Kit	$21.95
Living Trusts and Other Ways to Avoid Probate (3E)	$24.95
Mastering the MBE	$16.95
Nursing Homes and Assisted Living Facilities	$19.95
The Power of Attorney Handbook (5E)	$22.95
Quick Cash	$14.95
Seniors' Rights	$19.95
Sexual Harassment Your Guide to Legal Action	$18.95:
Sisters-in-Law	$16.95
The Social Security Benefits Handbook (4E)	$18.95
Social Security Q&A	$12.95
Starting Out or Starting Over	$14.95
Teen Rights (and Responsibilities) (2E)	$14.95
Unmarried Parents' Rights (and Responsibilities) (2E)	$19.95
U.S. Immigration and Citizenship Q&A	$18.95
U.S. Immigration Step by Step (2E)	$24.95
U.S.A. Immigration Guide (5E)	$26.95
What to Do—Before "I DO"	$14.95
The Wills, Estate Planning and Trusts Legal Kit	$26.95
Win Your Unemployment Compensation Claim (2E)	$21.95
Your Right to Child Custody, Visitation, & Support	$24.95